Rescue Your Own Damn Self

How to Write Your Own Feisty Fairy Tale, Slay Your Dragons & Live Sassily Ever After

Lori Mork

YGTMedia Co. Press Trade Paperback Edition

Published in Canada, for Global Distribution by YGTMedia Co.

www.ygtmedia.co/publishing

ISBN trade paperback: 978-1-989716-12-0

eBook: 978-1-989716-13-7

Audio Book: 978-1-989716-28-1

To order additional copies of this book: publishing@ygtmedia.co

Developmental Editing by Tania Jane Moraes-Vaz

Edited by Kelly Lamb and Christine Stock

Book design by Doris Chung

Cover design by Michelle Fairbanks

ePub & Kindle editions by Ellie Silpa

Author Photo by Shelly Fey

Illustration by HYPRLOOX

Printed in North America

Rescue Your Own Damn Self

Dedicated to...

All the badass babes out there who feel deeply, love fiercely, hurt, cry, have outbursts, have been told to settle down, and have thought they needed to find love or someone to fix them, love them, or rescue them.

To the queens who have always felt lost, waiting and hoping that some "happily ever after" will help them be found.

To the sexy goddesses who have felt the pressure to fit perfect molds, societal norms, or impossible ideals for body, heart, soul, and life.

To the hotties who are struggling to fit in, are challenged to find the answers, or just wishing they could be their fab-ass selves.

To the vixens ready to take life by the balls, be the narrator of their own fairy tale of life, and live sassily ever after!

Pass the wine, my fellow warrior princesses, we are on this epic journey together.

It's time to rescue your own damn self!

xoxo Lori

Introduction

Last year I turned forty-five. Gasp! I know, you may think I was dreading this age. But I wasn't! I was just coming off what was an upswing from what I thought was my "rock bottom." You know, the point where you think things can't possibly get any worse, but they shock you and actually DO?!

I remember that moment as clear as day. I was lying in my bed with my two dogs one night, and I took a deep breath, and began sobbing. *Why me? Why can't I find a prince? Why can't I catch a break? Why can't I win the lottery? Why can't I drink wine and eat whatever I want and still be skinny and lean? How did I get here? Why am I in the space of feeling so broken and hopeless?*

For about a month, I spiraled into this deep dark hole, this cold space where I was so tired, helpless, depressed, miserable, and lost, all the while thinking I couldn't go on if I didn't find some answers.

I knew I had to get my ass in gear and write my second book. You see, my first book helped women everywhere rock their bodies, break free of the diet and fitness culture, and just own what they've got! I was ready to write best seller number two. My new publisher was waiting patiently, yet with so much anticipation.

But I was broken. My creative tank was running on empty. Every time I looked at a page to jot down notes, my mind drew a blank. I had nothing left in me to give, nothing left to pour out. Every time I sat in front of my laptop, I sobbed, *Why me?* My mindset had me stuck. I continued to sit in the shitstorm and have a pity party for myself, while that feeling of *I just can't!* gnawed at my stomach. Raise your hand if you're feeling me on this one?

I put it all away. I was done. I had no wind in my sails. Nothing left to give. No energy to put into anything. Like most people who navigate heartbreak, loss, betrayal, and hurt—be it in their relationships, career, or friendships—true to the cliché we see in sitcoms and movies, I put on my pajamas, grabbed the remote, and embarked on a massive *My life sucks and I suck and love sucks* Netflix binge-fest. Every single movie I watched involved love, loss, heartbreak, sadness, love affairs, breakups, whirlwind romances, deceit, and despair. It was a forty-nine-hour marathon. It was a weekend-long event of tear-drenched tissues. My eyes were all swollen and puffy from moments I cried so hard I couldn't catch my breath. At times, I would yell at the TV; in other instances, I felt so much pain I couldn't move. I didn't shower. I didn't text or speak to anyone. Thankfully, for this epic meltdown, the fridge was stocked with massive amounts of Pinot Grigio (with ice, always my go-to).

As I approached the fiftieth hour of this pity party, I sat in the dark room with nothing but silence. Thoughts in my cluttered mind screamed:

Why can't I find my Prince Charming?

Why isn't Adam Sandler singing to me and telling me I am the one?

Why is my life not all sunshine and unicorns?

Why am I not stinkin' rich and living in a castle?

Where is my Fairy Godmother? Did she retire? Is she on strike?

Wait, what? *What the actual eff!* This is fake. This is television. These are fables. This is the nonsense I have been fed my whole life.

I dragged myself to the shower (and cried one last time). Then I opened my laptop and started writing and writing and writing. My fingers kept clicking, or as I call it, chicken pecking. I type fast!

I looked back on my last four-and-a-half decades and how I got to this place. The trials and tribulations I endured. The ups and the downs. The highs and the lows. I thought back to all the years I was fed a web of misinformation from Disney princess shows to romantic comedies with hunky leading men. Was it all bullshit? Was there more to this whole "being saved and living happily ever after" that I was missing?

I began to get angry. I had full-blown rage at the tears I shed in thinking that no white knight on a horse was coming to help me, and for all of the moments I waited to have some switch turn on in my brain to make me think I could walk through life, singing and dancing merrily. I thought about the poor decisions I had made in relationships due to my lack of self-confidence, self-worth, and self-esteem. I thought back to every sleepless night I had worrying about shit that didn't matter, things I couldn't control, and things that were never to be explained. I thought about the narrative in my head around how I was supposed to be, do, and act. How I was supposed to show up. My mind was racing, my head was spinning. I thought about all the times I believed the pot of gold would just magically appear at the end of the storms I was enduring, only to never find that rainbow.

Then I thought about the fact that this wasn't just *my* problem! I wasn't the only one sitting in madness and confusion. In fact, I had seen thousands of other women throughout my thirty years as a fitness and wellness coach who were also on the "struggle train" with no stops in sight. I thought about all the women I have witnessed in my long career who are broken, upset, sad, depressed, and at their wits' end for being so hard on themselves. I have seen countless women with low self-esteem, very little self-worth, and zero self-acceptance. I have watched, and continue to watch, the vicious cycle we, as women, continue to put ourselves through. The nonstop race we continue to run. And newsflash—the race isn't even ours to begin with. It's a race with time, society, and ideals. The comparison games, the judgments—of oneself and others—the self-deprecation, the self-loathing, the self-bullying.

The "not living our fullest lives," often stuck on the hamster wheel, never finding true happiness or success. The juggling and feeling "less than" when any of the balls drop, and man, do they drop! We just keep spinning our wheels in a world that keeps setting us up to fail. I think about the friends I have had who weren't happy in their sex lives, who were in dead-end relationships because they just didn't have the courage to say, "I'm out of here!" Nor did they have the audacity to claim their dreams, their desires, their wants and needs. I've watched endless numbers of women (and men too) experience feeling this way. Though this book tends to focus on the ladies, nobody is exempt from this vicious cycle. It affects every human being who keeps thinking some perfect life is supposed to exist and is afraid to talk about the "messy parts."

Remember the fairy tale? You know, the one where the princess loses her shoe, then finds her Prince Charming for life? Or the one where the sad, shunned princess bites an apple, falls under a spell, then gets kissed by some random dude and becomes alive and happy? Or the one where the babe is a fish, then just falls in love and finds her legs? Are we supposed to believe all these goddesses just magically live happily ever after? Thanks for the low expectations, Disney! Ugh!

Or what about the endless numbers of romantic comedies we flock to watch in the theater (or on Netflix for all the youngsters out there), where we see two very attractive lead actors meet, fall hard, love harder, and come together for life. They ride off into the sunset, every single time! Our reality is surely royally screwed up if we think some rich guy marries the prostitute and it's all sunshine and roses for life! Honey, nobody is coming to save you. This isn't *Pretty Woman* or *Maid in Manhattan* or whatever other movie that got these ideals stuck in your head. Am I saying you shouldn't have hopes and dreams? Of course not. You should dream, with some realism, and they should be YOUR dreams—in relationships with yourself, others, and how you live your life. It's time to rescue your own damn self, straighten your crown, and stop chasing and living a life designed by others and their expectations.

Happily ever after . . . does it really exist?

What if that story line is supposed to be more about us women being our own damn saviors?

What if *we* are actually the ones with the tools—the pen in our hand—learning, living, laughing, stumbling, making mistakes, and writing our own damn story?

What if *your* fairy tale is supposed to have bumps, bruises, tears, loss, gain, hilarious embarrassing moments of nonsense, gaining the pounds, then losing the pounds?

What if *your* romantic comedy doesn't always have the hot

guy at the end choosing you? Or heck, maybe you decide that YOU don't want to pick him, and you get a cute dog instead?

What if the happily ever after was not actually just about being happy? What if all emotions and life's lessons contribute to our epic fables?

Maybe it was time for me to sit back and reflect on my years in this messy life of mine. Like a fine wine, I had aged well and had seen my share of some pretty epic stuff. I had years of hating on my body, being sad because of how some random dude treated me, and always stressing about baseless shit!

That was when the lightbulb turned on. The magic pixie dust rained on me and covered me in all its sparkle and glitter! I had this aha moment of *Gurl, it's time to pull up those big girl panties and write your own damn fairy tale of how you finally learned that life was about owning it all—the sad chapters, the deaths, the messy bits—and learning from them. Taking those silly parts and laughing your ass off and making it okay to do dumb shit!*

Maybe it was time to finally put pen to paper and write my own Netflix series of ways I learned that life is more about living and less about perfection. It's about embracing your imperfections and owning the heck out of them and sharing them with pride! It's time to end the facade that we can't have massive mess-ups and epic failures yet still rise up with resilience and strength and keep fighting.

You had the sword all along, Princess, to slay the dragon and save your kingdom!

What if these truth bombs, stories, mic-drop moments, and lessons learned with all the crazy and chaotic madness were also meant to be documented and screamed from the rooftops to younger generations? In these messy stories, I was writing my own happily ever after. These were my "if only I knew then what I know now" epiphanies. In that instant, I knew that I needed to share this story with EVERY woman, no matter what stage of life they're in. Twenties, thirties, forties, fifties—heck, it's not too late for us to laugh and grow together in our sixties, seventies, and beyond. **It's never too late for us to rescue our own damn selves!**

Let this book be your personal manifesto and cheeky anthem that you use to create your own badass fairy tale, where a sad maiden in a tower who is waiting to be rescued by some prince finds out she had the tools she needed all along to rescue herself. She discovers that not only is she a fierce warrior, but **she is the fire-breathing dragon who can take on the world!**

But we aren't going to wake up breathing fire overnight. Mastering that takes time. Trust me, it took me forty-five years! Heck, I am still evolving and growing every damn day! These sassy solutions, truth bombs, guidelines, mantras, mottos, rules to live by, rants and raves—whatever you want to call them—can serve as a guide to help us take one step at a time on this yellow brick road we are strolling on. These funny stories and anecdotes can serve as little potions and pixie dust to help create the magic we all need to live an amazing life and finally feel confident in our own skin. Let them be a way of being in control of all that is our own Academy Award-winning movie!

Just a heads-up: I swear a ton, and I can't promise that I toned it down in this book, as hard as I tried. The voice in my head says, "Lori, ladies shouldn't swear!" Yeah, yeah, that's a myth right there. I tried to leave out the F-bombs and take the swearing down a notch in this book, but they do creep in, so think of these swear words as passionate posting or me clearing my throat chakra.

Let's go on this quest together and finally live sassily ever after!

Who Am I? What's My Story?

This book covers my life's journey—all my crazy stories, escapades, and roller coaster rides. Yep, you get it all in here! I hold nothing back. Consider me your cool older sister who buys you booze when you aren't old enough. The best friend who pours the wine and gives the best advice and the raciest and most inappropriate guidance. That random stranger in the washroom at the night-club who hands you a tampon or wipes your tears and tells you that the jerk you are with doesn't deserve your hotness. I'm your hype girl! Your online bestie who everyone knows they'll get the goods and truth from and who always has the best time! But let me give you the short and sweet version of who the heck I am, how broken I was, and how the hell I rescued myself, then we can have some fun together!

I, Lori Mork, was born November 13, 1975, weighing eight pounds and zero ounces. Who knew that would be the very first time society considered me a "plump" human!

Let's insert more than two decades of being chunky, struggling with low self-esteem, low self-worth, and doing things for people just so they would like me. Wanting to be someone else, wanting a better life, always striving to find "what's next?" or "what's better?" and "my true love and happiness."

When I was a teen, most of the poor and often fucked-up choices I made were an attempt at seeking approval, acceptance, and validation from others. It was a cry for some kind of attention from people who used, abused, and didn't give a crap about me!

My name is Lori, and I am a self-proclaimed romantic comedy movie junkie! I have watched them sixty-five billion times each. Still as an adult I'm obsessed with all the classic fairy tales. I use words like "soul mates" and "true love" on a daily basis. I love hard, I give hard, I feel hard, and then, like the sandcastle, I eventually crumble.

In the most recent version of myself, I stopped believing the nonsense and wiped my tears. **I nixed the people pleasing and**

decided to grab a sword and stop being the helpless princess! #causethatsbullshit (See, I swear, sorry!)

So, I fixed my crown. It is still super crooked and tarnished, but now I choose to write my life story with the premise being "Lori's romantic comedy, action adventure, magical-mess of goodness, sadness, and madness." Sounds like a best screenplay winner! And ya know what, you can write your story too! You can produce and direct your own award-winning best actor performance!

I hope this book will give you all the clarity you desire. Maybe it makes you laugh a little and sob a little because of all the bull you've endured. I hope you stop waiting for someone to save you and truly witness the magic and power that lies within you. Write your own fairy tale. Because nobody, and I mean nobody puts (insert your name) in a corner! *Dirty Dancing,* anyone?

How to Read This Book

In this book you will find three types of chapters. You don't need to read it in chronological order. You can if you want to, but honestly, I wrote this book with the intention of it being a pick-me-up, pep talk, tough love from your bestie that you can simply plug into every day. For the busy moms out there, lock yourself in the bathroom, or heck, a pantry or closet, away from your crazy kids, and quickly skim two or three short and sassy chapters to find some solace and sanity! #whenyaknowyaknow Or read it intuitively by choosing a random chapter or page . . . or read it in order, the choice is yours. I like to mix things up to keep things spicy!

Lori's Life Lessons

The bulk of this epic novel is filled with these types of "chapters."

A sprinkling of pixie dust or magic potions in glorious chunks throughout this book.

Oprah-style aha moments.

Times you just say out loud, "Fuck yeah!" (*language, Lori*); "Heck yeah, gurl!"; "Preach, sista!"

It's all the shit I've learned, in little stories, takeaways, thoughts, experiences, and realizations. I swear these "chapters" should have been my bible of all things life.

Shit I wish I knew thirty or forty years ago!

Things I wish I was told much sooner to help me navigate and not feel so lost in this magical forest of my existence.

Ways in which I, Lori Mork, have learned from my own missteps.

Observations I witnessed from my clients, or friends' stories of inspiration and hilariousness, which I then lumped into a bundle of goodness and nicknamed "The book to help you rescue your damn self!"

Disclaimer: I've changed everyone's names to keep their secrets safe with me. I don't want anyone to die of embarrassment as others read about their wild escapades—or their vaginas!

Fairy Tale Facades

Ah, the fairy tale. Growing up, reading those bedtime stories, then watching them on screen, and dreaming of that magical castle, that handsome prince to save us, or that love of a lifetime seemed like a dream come true. Boy, did that set us up for epic relationship failures and unrealistic expectations. A facade is a front. An outside appearance that kind of tricks us and doesn't tell us what's real or reality!

Like that handsome prince the girl just meets, who somehow saved her from her life of chaos, even though they haven't spoken more than ten words. But we buy it! Because it feels secure. It feels safe. It feels like we are taken care of. Primal, human, survival needs and instincts. Heck, I've been in relationships where I have overlooked so many red flags because I was dreaming of that happily ever after with my prince. WTF moments of trying to make sense of the nonsense or explain the crap we were told by the fairy tale narrative, which was sold to us by all the publishing and movie moguls (though I still love those movies!). I'm not saying these fairy tales need to be abolished in some tower, locked away, never to be read or seen again, but what if we could make fun of them a little, point out the facades, and then take a sharp turn. What if I gave you **Lori's spin on how it shoulda played out?!**

Come on these little fairy tale adventures with me, with a whole lotta *Lori sass* added!

Rewrite the Rom-Com

I love a good old romantic comedy!

I laugh at it, cry at it, and sit back and think, "Oh, I can't wait for this to go down in my life!" Then one day I realized that it's all bullshit!

Most of what I was watching was setting me up for unrealistic expectations of love, romance, and life. Most of it was smoke being blown by some dragon of complete bullshittery.

Bullshittery is what we are fed and what is written in bright lights on massive billboards!

Girl meets boy, who is always a stallion hunk or a man with a wicked English accent (oh hey, Hugh Grant!). They fall in love after just a few hours, or sometimes minutes, and live happily ever after.

Aw, life is so easy, isn't it?! No! Life is not easy. Love is not easy. Romance takes work. I laugh at some of the nonsense we women want to believe or aspire to make happen for us.

I shed light on some shit that I know just wouldn't happen and add a little **Lori's plot twist** to them. Like how would I like to see this really play out, or what's the realistic version of this love connection?

It's funny, enlightening, and just good times to sit back with the popcorn in a comfy set of pj's and be reminded love is great and all, but it's time for some transparency about what's really gonna go down when that man is standing on your doorstep saying you "complete" him!

Enough chit-chat already! Let's get this show on the road! Let's go on a journey to return the ring to the lords! Let's head to Grandma's house and try to avoid the nasty wolf! Let's get our own damn ladder and climb down out of our tower. Hell, let's install a nice glass elevator! Let's go on a mission to figure out this so-called life and make it easier to know it's not about skipping along into the sunset in a beautiful tulle gown. And that's okay!

Seatbelts fastened? It's gonna be a fun and funky ride!

Once upon a time, this hot babe . . .

Welcome to the Shitshow...
Embrace Your Crazy!

We are all a little loopy.

A little off kilter.

Bonkers.

Mad.

Quirky.

Messy.

But I have a little secret: the best babes are!

We are all just navigating and making do in this chaotic comedy of a life we have. I legit have three sweatshirts that say "hot mess" on them. A disclaimer of sorts to anyone who comes into contact with me to be forewarned.

I don't do "normal" very well. Never have. To me, normal was always too safe. I'm like a "fly by the seat of my pants" kinda girl (*Pretty Woman*, anyone? More on that romantic comedy fail later!). I "do" and then think later, which gets me into a shit ton of trouble, but it also helps me find some amazing success and have fun experiences. I prefer being the round peg trying to fit into a square hole. Go against the grain. Swim upstream, usually without a paddle!

I was rebranding my business and needed a photoshoot to showcase my new self and the services I offer. I could have played it safe and done the "typical" fitness coach photoshoot with me in some black bra top and black lululemon pants pretending to be a badass workout queen. Instead, I got into a pink tutu and Cinderella heels and strutted the streets of downtown Vancouver. I drank wine in a bathtub of donuts and jumped on a bed with fruit loops flying around me. This was me, in all my glory. It was as ME as it could get in a photoshoot. And sure enough, those pictures have my essence, my energy, and my personality in them. They're truly me! Take it or leave it! (Most take it—I'm #funasfuck)

Growing up, I was always told, "Lori, you're so crazy!" And they meant that label as a negative. But what if being crazy means you are authentically you? Own that crazy, be unique, and ditch the thoughts that crazy means psycho. Let's embrace the wild side of the word. Never change who you are to please others. Keep it 100 percent real in your thoughts, actions, and feelings. It shows you are passionate. Some of the craziest souls possess more passion in their pinky fingers than others have in their whole bodies. When you embrace your crazy—whatever that looks and feels like—you become a dreamer. You think up shit no one else would dare to dream about. And you make it happen! You make the impossible possible! Crazy people aren't afraid to stand up for themselves or for what is right. When you can embrace your crazy, you also stand up for what you need and want and aren't afraid to ask for it. You become bolder, more certain of who you are. You become unshakable because you've already embraced your inner weirdo and found a fierce connection with your emotions. Like you legit give a fuck about a lot. You become this feeler, highly in tune with all the emotions that run deep within.

 **#storytime**   **Jessie's Girl**

(Rick Springfield, anyone?) I'm not allowed to post lyrics so let's just say Jessie is a friend . . . My client Jessie was always told she was crazy. She was a hippie, who wore outfits no one else would. Her amazing shining light was beaming beyond what others thought of her. But she struggled. She pretended she was okay being made fun of. She often joked about owning her crazy, but the stigma of being different hung over her and made her feel less than. She sunk into a great depression. I lost the Jessie I once knew. She conformed to dressing how others thought she should. She didn't make fun and quirky comments to make others laugh anymore. Her light was not only dimmed, it was burned the fuck out. For years, she carried on this way until one day I asked her why she needed to change for others. Why did she need to hide what others perceived as crazy? I loved crazy! And I was empowered by her crazy. Sign me up for the wild, crazy train. Toot! Toot!

I relit Jessie's crazy flame, and we were the dynamic duo back in action together! I took my crazy up another three notches and really owned my uniqueness. I started to dye my hair the colors of the rainbow without fear of labels. When someone would tell me, "Lori, you are so crazy!" I always turned it into a positive. I even started using the word "crazy" for positivity and light. I stopped apologizing to others for my sass or differentness. Sure, embracing your crazy sounds like you become this handful, but if people can't handle you with all your crazed energy, find new people with bigger hands to surround yourself with!

To this day, I still know Jessie. I still coach her. We often have "crazy parties" or "sassy psycho bashes." When two badasses, a duet of unapologetic hotties, get together to unleash their crazy, you better believe this results in one of the most kick-ass times ever!

Embrace your crazy, babe! The crazy ones are always the ones changing the world, because nobody here is going to wait for the prince to climb the tower to make them "sane." Here, we take life by the balls, and we own our wackiness!

Rescue your own damn self by embracing your unique blend of crazy, kooky, and weird, and live sassily ever after!

Screw Society's Impossible Body Ideals!

....

Let's reflect on the nonsense I watched on the old "boob tube" in my youth that ensured I would have a lifetime of absurd realities contributing to my insanely low body image!

I'm a '70's and '80's wild child, so, if you are with me in your forties and fifties, you may remember all the amazing different shapes and sizes that the most popular TV shows portrayed. *Charlie's Angels* had lots of different-sized women . . . wait . . . umm . . . who was the curvy, chunky angel again? There wasn't one! Okay, what about *Three's Company*? Nope, Janet and Chrissy surely weren't more than a size zero! Well, *The Dukes of Hazzard* had to have a more realistic body image . . . oh goodness, no thunder thighs were fitting into those Daisy Dukes. *Dallas, Dynasty, Happy Days*, etc., all had countless tiny frames with minimal body fat and zero muscles. Epic fail!

Okay, that era sucked for unrealistic body ideals, but the '90s had to have gotten better, right? Shows like *Friends, Saved by the Bell, Dawson's Creek* must have presented more diverse body sizes. No? *Beverly Hills, 90210* and *Melrose Place* were . . . not filled with anyone but skinny models. Where were the more muscular, full-figured girls who rocked their curves on TV? Missing in action yet again!

Throughout our lifetimes, we were conditioned to believe in the "one-size-fits-all-body," and present-day media hasn't changed much either. Everywhere we turn, we are bombarded with pictures of the ideal body, unrealistic body types, and some bullshit that the "cute hot girl" always gets the dreamy lead hunk!

I might need some tissues to write this next story. Tanya was one of my long-term clients, way back in the day when I first started training people. When the internet didn't exist and we met in gyms and wrote programs out on napkins or scrap paper. She was this amazing forty-something-year-old woman with curves for days. She was stunning. A smile to light up a room. Everyone loved her, but Tanya had her demons. She was the first client I worked with who had struggled with such severe anorexia and bulimia that I needed to communicate with her therapist and her doctors during our training. We worked out together for about five years. I say "about" because most of the time she was in and out of hospital wards specializing in eating disorders. I know I've been lucky to have never struggled with an eating disorder myself, but sadly my career has brought forth hundreds, if not thousands, who were not so fortunate. And Tanya had it the worst I had seen. (Many of us can relate to disordered eating patterns or struggle with the head games around dieting and food obsessions!) When we would talk about her *why,* it would often come back to the same things: impossible society ideals and standards. Back then it was magazines and TV spewing the images at us. But Tanya had been a model, actress, and divorced three times. Nothing she could ever do made her happy in her life and with her body.

There was no underlying reasoning behind the disorder like past abuse or childhood trauma. It was literally all about trying to fit some mold set out by society. I didn't get it, though. You see, I saw something different than she did. She was stunning, and her body was beautiful. But we as women, myself included, can sometimes fail to see what's in front of us. I remember asking her why she couldn't be content in her own skin. Why couldn't she just live life and be happy? And I will never forget her answer as long as I live, and it's probably why, to this day, almost twenty years later, I still don't have issues with my body in the extremes that some do. I still give a damn about what models look like, or what is shown on TV shows or in movies or magazines. But I know it's not realistic. And I know it's not *my* "real."

The last time I saw my client (here come the tears again), she was 89 pounds. As I sat next to her hospital bed, the prognosis was that her organs had cried out "enough is enough!" She was still that ray of light she had always been. She still kept me laughing with her amazing jokes and stories. But the very last thing I remember her telling me before I left was this: "You create your own ideals. Don't let anyone tell you that you aren't beautiful just as you are. When you accept where you are now and are okay with it, you stop striving for something that doesn't exist. This thought if we just keep pushing, we will get to some impossible ideal. I've been shooting for this for far too long and I'm exhausted! It doesn't mean you don't have ways you want to be better. But please just know that you are good enough just as you are, now. You can then sit in the moment knowing it doesn't matter who looks like what, or who has a smaller ass or tighter abs. Or what some dumb scale says. You are you, and you are fabulous! I wish I had known decades ago that I was good enough, and that those stupid images I was fed shouldn't have been allowed to convince me otherwise."

I thought of Tanya the other day as I passed the rack of magazines at the local grocery store. You know the ones at the checkout that show the perfect models, spew impossible dieting solutions, and cry out "you aren't good enough!" My eyes filled with tears instantly. Because the world hasn't changed in the last twenty years, and it won't be changing any time soon. It's time to shake things up and reclaim your body, your ideals, and do what feels good for you. Live in a way that feels true to you. It shows up in all other areas of your life, trust me!

I wish this fairy tale had a happy ending, but Tanya passed away peacefully in that very same hospital bed where she said her last words to me. And to this day, I don't read any of those magazines, and I carefully choose to watch a variety of shows that showcase more diversity in terms of body types.

Rescue your own damn self from society's unattainable and pathetic body ideals that are complete bullshit, and live sassily ever after!

To my dear Tanya, and to anyone who has lost a loved one due to an eating disorder or the complications that arise from them: rest in peace, my friend. Tanya, you were and always will be one of the most beautiful women I have known, and I was so lucky to meet you.

Just Start!

We all gotta start somewhere. "Beginner's luck" is when you start something new for the first time, get lucky, and are fantastic or a natural at it!

You're a newbie at it!

Like the famous Madonna song "Like a Virgin," where allll those new sensations are stirred up . . . mmm . . . sorry, what was I sayin'? Right, just start!

"Just Do It" is the slogan from Nike used to empower us to just start, just begin. But it's not that easy, I get it. It's scary to jump into new things, start new adventures, tackle a new journey. Scary as shit! In fact, fear usually holds us back from ever taking that leap to begin with. We usually have this overwhelming fear of failure, or worse, of just not being "good enough."

About twenty years ago, I decided I was going to take up golf. When I put my mind to something, the perfectionist in me jumps right in. I was gonna be the female Tiger Woods. As I hit the green, I was about to have my ass handed to me. I was terrible! I had zero patience to learn anything. I was left-handed and golfing with a bunch of right-handers. My ego took a huge hit. But I took the risk; I put in the effort to try. Now, my story shouldn't be inspirational, since I have yet to return to the old golf course since storming off the green that one sucky time! But it brings me to more inspiring stories of "beginning."

 **January 1—New Year's Resolutioners' Central**

We know this time of year. Time to get that dream body. Time to undertake an intense workout regimen at the local fitness club. #beastmode All in! But it's a scary time in a big gym. There is a lot of intimidating equipment, and it can be daunting to get the death glares from those around us. But I promise you that once you get through that initial petrified feeling of entering those front doors that first day, it gets easier. And it becomes a habit. And it definitely feels a lot less scary. It becomes routine, and before you know it, you are the one eyeing up the newbies when the following new year rolls around!

Beginning or starting, or heck, starting over, doesn't have to just be about your fitness journey or undertaking a new hobby. It can be quitting your job and venturing into a new career path.

 **How Tracy Got Her Groove Back— The Saga Continues . . . or Begins**

One of my favorite stories is that of my client Tracy who got a divorce at age sixty. She was terrified to date again. She would not put herself out there. She had been burned by husband one. She hadn't had to date since she was eighteen! Dating sites didn't exist back then, and just an FYI: Dating sites scare the fuck out of me! I hear the horror stories from my girlfriends, and I am more terrified of dating sites than a fire-breathing dragon!

Dating sites didn't exist back in my dating days (THANK GOD!). Heck, there wasn't even electricity on the computer back then (okay, there was electricity, but not Plenty of Fish—or sharks!). My lack of knowledge of them, and the fact it wasn't me doing the jumping, made it easy to push her on the daily to get on those sites! I wouldn't dare tell her I myself was frightened of Tinder, Bumble, Elite Singles, etc. *WTF—how are we even navigating all of these?!*

I even told her I would help her with her profile. (You know, the lies everyone tells about themselves to make it seem like they are important, hot, rich, and ready to mingle!) No way! She was against it. But she was alone, and lonely. One day she came to one of our sessions with tears in her eyes and said, "I want to meet my new love, someone I can spend the next twenty or thirty years with." We filled out her online profile with that very statement. She finally did it, with me as her life preserver.

Sometimes, we need help starting, beginning, taking that leap! And wanna know the happily ever after? Tracy and Craig just celebrated their tenth anniversary last month, and got married eight years ago, two years after meeting on that very dating site, with that very dating profile that I wrote with her.

Just start! You never know where the fairy tale ending will be!

The biggest take away from these two stories is this: *Don't jump in the deep end, go to the wading pool first!* Just start where you are and ease in.

When I took up golf, I definitely didn't prepare myself for it. I didn't take lessons. I went with a bunch of random friends who hadn't the first clue on how to properly swing a club, nor were they even that good at it themselves. I jumped without a net, and that's when I quit!

Be the person who tests the water and has a gentle entry in. Just the tip! Oh wait, that's another chapter. Just the toe dip?

Rescue your own damn self by beginning, starting, just doing it, and that will be that first step on your journey to living sassily ever after!

Eat Pray Love

Leave it to Julia Roberts to star in some of the most epic "pull at your heartstrings" movies that molded and shaped my completely delusional concept of finding love and living some notion of happily ever after!

That being said, the concept of *Eat Pray Love* has my heart all wrapped up with a big, endearing bow, ready to burst!

But as I watched it for the seventeenth time (okay, seventieth), I hit pause and had a "back up, sista" moment.

Wait, for those who haven't watched this heart-warmer, let's get ya caught up on this movie's plot.

Girl is at a crossroads in life. She leaves her unhappy marriage, but she still can't find love. She has totally lost herself and hates her life! She finds herself sobbing hysterically while curled up on the cold, hard floor of her apartment, unable to function (Amen, drop the mic, been there, my friend!).

So, she picks her sad and sorry self up, sells everything, and goes on an epic journey to find:

- Amazing, tasty food (Italy)
- Internal beliefs and prayer (India)
- The love of her life (Bali)

While this all sounds fine and dandy, I could barely get dressed when I was at my low point and had my mental breakdown, much less board a plane across oceans. My bank account laughed its ass off at me with the thought of being able to afford Italy, India, and Bali from the negative checking account balance and "savings account." What's that?

But I wanted to find myself! I wanted to learn about enjoyment of food, a higher power, and love. I wanted to get up off the floor and stop crying, damn it!

When we hit rock bottom, and it surely comes, sometimes multiple times for us, how the hell do we eat, pray, and love again?!

What if this whole magical concept could be found locally and on a daily basis?

What if every single day we ensured we found and lived this triple threat for life?!

EAT

What if on the daily, you made sure you ate only the foods you liked and that made you feel good? Legit, how hard is that? What if you chose food you actually liked the taste of? And took the time to sit down to meals and enjoy every single bite. Stopped thinking less about what it was doing for your exterior appearance, made it all about nourishing from within, and finding enjoyment again in eating. Not from some diet guru who tells you that you *have to* eat egg whites, gross and slimy white fish, and the latest trendy "super" foods. Kale? Yuck, blech!

Sure, in the movie, being in Italy was all about pizza, pasta, and wine in excess. Are we sure this was Italy and not Heaven? I promise you if you block out all the noise, don't have anything "off limits," and just listen to your body, it will pick the good things. Sure, some days this will be chicken parmesan with a heavy sauce, but most days it will be smoothies packed with antioxidants. Trust me!

PRAY

I am not saying we need to go to church every day or to even believe in the concept of God, whatever that looks like to you. Prayer to me is believing in some kind of higher power. The Universe, God, the guru, the thought that somehow, somewhere if we just find silence or stillness in our minds, we can allow our thoughts to surface, release, and believe in something. This could be gratitude for those of you who don't have someone you pray to, or it could be trusting in this *vibe* and *energy* around us and taking a moment every single day to just BE.

LOVE

We all want to BE loved. We are always searching for someone, anyone to love us. That attractive prince, that hottie, that stallion.

That person of our dreams. I liked this concept in the movie, but really, babe, in life, let's make this about showing up daily for ourselves. Let's love our own damn selves. PERIOD! Looking and searching for love in an external source or person is a recipe for disappointment and maybe even disaster. Without love for yourself, no other love can be enough to be let in through those castle gates! So, I like the love part of this one being only about the most important person on the planet—YOUR DAMN SELF!

"Eat Gratitude Self-Love" is better, but it doesn't flow off the tongue as easily, so we'll stick with the original Eat Pray Love.

Rescue your own damn self on a daily basis, and live sassily ever after! You don't need to jet off to Italy, India, and Bali to find true love, joy, and inner peace. It's within you. It always has been. Now pass the pasta and Pinot!

Hey, Soul Sista!

....

To me, the *soul* is who we are deep down, beneath the surface, without labels or titles. Who we are when everything else is stripped away. Who we are at our core.

We constantly talk about finding our "soul mate." Finding that one person to "complete" us. Thanks *Jerry* freakin' *Maguire*! (More on that romantic comedy shitstorm later!)

What if we found our own damn soul mate and realized we were the key to a lifetime of happiness all along? It wasn't an external source. What would it feel like to stop searching for outside people for love and realize that nurturing your own inner soul is what will help you write your phenomenal fairy tale?!

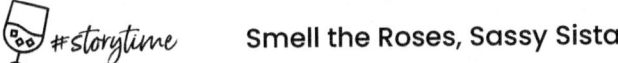 **#storytime   Smell the Roses, Sassy Sista**

Do you actually take time to smell the roses? Or in my case, to slow down and take in all that is around us, going deep within to reflect, pause, and simply feel our way through life and sink into each moment? In 2021, I set a goal or intention to watch more sunsets. It sounds like a weird New Year's Resolution, but it was needed. I used to walk my dog up on this hill where I lived. Everyone's evening walk would be the perfect time to see the most glorious sunsets. I would stop. And for just a moment, I could block out the whole world. I could sit and in an instant, any worries I had were gone . . . poof! Magically nonexistent. That sunset was pretty incredible. I used that time to be still. To be present. To be with myself. And this beautiful sun would set and then return the next day to shine again. Sounds corny, but when I moved, I lost this daily treasure. I stopped seeing sunsets. And I lost a little bit of that connection with my soul. To start this again, maybe I could return to finding myself. So, I committed to adding this back in, and within just a few of those glorious sunsets, I felt more like myself again. I let go of anxiety, released some emotions, and found my own damn soul mate in myself. It was ME all along. Time alone with myself "completed" my own damn story. I found the missing character, a.k.a. hot princess, sitting right here!

Alone time is all we need, babe. It doesn't have to be a sunset; maybe you're more of a sunrise person. Running a bath is my second favorite reason to be naked. Wait, what was I talking about? Oh right, being still and calm. But be sure to lock the damn door or your toddler is gonna be shitting on the toilet next to you! Or your teen will come in and bother you for a ride somewhere.

Time alone helps you block out the noise of day-to-day

events. I, for one, have come to appreciate the simple things . . . like my Starbucks refresher or Sephora bath bombs. Find your simple pleasure, whatever that is. Just dig deep to appreciate the now, in time with yourself, and your amazing soul!

Okay, I know. Some of us loathe the thought of being alone. The word "alone" has this stigma around it like you are some "loner" or "loser." Some of us get antsy just thinking about being that person who is operating solo! Like going to the movies on their own. I am guilty of feeling sorry for that one person sitting there in the dark theater alone. Or should I flip the way I look at it? Are they actually the one to be envious of? Since they feel good and enjoy their own company, they are their own soul mate. Or that person who sits in the restaurant eating their meal as their own damn date! No phone, no conversation, just a person and their food. I always looked at it as feeling bad for them since they weren't with anyone, but maybe I was wrong all along and they got it right?!

 #storytime   **Candace Craves Company**

My client Candace was the queen of judging people who were by themselves. She was terrified of dying alone. She would joke about being with her cats when we all found her cold, dead body. But it was a real feeling she had. You see, she struggled with self-esteem her whole life. She was codependent and never single. She would get out of one relationship, only to dive quickly into another. She invested in tons of therapy one year after a traumatic breakup. Her therapist told her to start being alone more. To take one whole year for some self-exploration. Fly solo! (Don't Google this term, it's not the same as what I mean here. I don't mean masturbation; that's another chapter!) So, Candace booked a trip to Mexico for spring break, like masturbating all by herself! Gasp! We were judging her before she even left the gates at the airport. We thought for sure she would wind up falling for someone she met in the buffet line and fall right back into her old pattern. But when she came back, her smile was infectious. She was lighter, brighter, and just liked herself more. It was just what the doctor ordered for her to realize she didn't need that hot Tom Cruise-like bartender to complete her, she completed her own damn self! Heck, her standards were even higher now, since she knew she was the bomb and deserved only the best souls to surround her. Loving herself meant that the next man she would let into her life would have a very high bar to reach for or live up to!

Life just flows more effortlessly, more naturally, when we find more gratitude for the time we have on this earth within our beautiful selves, and less time to think some charming cutie is going to be the answer to our lifelong happiness.

Do I still believe in soul mates? Damn straight! #ICYMI (which my teen tells me means "in case you missed it!"), I am a romantic comedy junkie, my friends. But I do believe we have to be okay in our own souls before we go searching for any other suckers to share our lives with!

Rescue your own damn self by finding your soul, which in turn means "completing" yourself (and actually rescuing yourself from Tom Cruise jumping on your couch!), and live sassily ever after!

Truth Bombs Are da Bomb!

Do you swear to tell the truth, the whole truth, and nothing but the truth, so help you, Goddess?

"You can't handle the truth!" (Another epic Tom Cruise movie, anyone?)

Sure, maybe we can't absorb the honest stuff, but we all need a girlfriend in our life who is the bearer of all things gospel!

Friends who drop #truthbombs, even when you don't wanna hear it. Even when you are in some shitstorm thinking it's a good idea. Friends who stand face-to-face with you and say, "The fuck you are!" Those are the sweet souls you keep around for life. So, in the pursuit to rescue our own damn selves, you will see that sometimes we need that Thelma and Louise dynamic to assist in the saving of us! We got their back; they got ours! A team effort! Get the shovel, but just don't drive off the cliff in your car! (*Thelma and Louise*, remember?!)

Lipstick on your teeth. I got you!

Making a big mistake or screwup that everyone else ignores or looks away from without commenting? Nope. Not this kind of friend. We tell it like it is.

This friend pours the wine and waves her finger saying, "Gurl, you need to wake the fuck up!"

This sista doesn't fake anything—except orgasms with her crazy ex (*When Harry Met Sally*, anyone?). She knows you not only can handle it, but you can also throw it right back at her with your own truths and #facts when she needs it.

#storytime   **The Coral Yoga Pants**

I was at the local lululemon store about eight years ago when I realized I had *that* kinda friend. I was there with three hotties from my girl squad. I came out of the change room ready to *work it*, in the most amazing coral leggings. They were neon pink and orange and bright AF. I was hot! #itwasnot

My one girlfriend exclaimed, "Wow, those are amazing!"

The second one looked me up and down a few times and said, "Those pants are perfect for you."

Sounds great, right?! Well . . . from ten feet across the store, I see my third friend sprinting, lunging, screaming . . . almost in slow motion, "Hell no! Girl, your big booty ain't meant for coral, like no, no, no!"

As the other two "liars" smirked in agreement, both unwilling to tell me the truth, that third friend had my heart—and my back. She refused to let this sexy butt look terrible in public. Did I take it personally? Nope! Did I take those coral pants off, never to speak of them again? Heck to the yes! You see, we need that one friend who just blurts out the truth. You know they love you, you know they don't want to ever hurt you, but you know they also don't want you looking like a fool by rocking neon coral pants when you have a massive trunk full of junk!

You should never be afraid of telling your friends or loved ones the truth. Or of just being raw and real with them and knowing they would give you the same. And receiving constructive feedback in return. In fact, feedback saves lives. I truly do believe that. Or in this case, those genuine and truth-telling comments from my friend saved my sexy ass from those awful coral pants!

 #storytime   **Running Away with My Dream Man**

We've all been there. At least once in our lives. We meet this amazing guy. He is our Prince Charming! He is our soul mate. The one we will live happily ever after with. We are consumed by them, clouded by love, ass-deep in passion. Well, this happened for one of my besties (I am not naming names, so let's call her Karen). She met a guy who was a capital L for "loser." She would rave to me about him nonstop, but he was toxic, he was terrible. He wasn't that attractive and couldn't carry a real conversation. Let's just say she had "big dick syndrome." You're laughing right now, but y'all know what I'm talking about. The type of dude who can cast a spell over you to believe he's the king of the kingdom, but in reality, it's just the eight to ten inches waving some magic wand over your sanity!

I bit my tongue and allowed her to have her hot sex, amazing romps, more hot sex, and the initial high of the relationship. But one day, about a year in (I know, I let her have a lot of orgasms knowing it *should not* and *could not* go anywhere else), she texted me, "I love him, and we're running away together. We're going to buy a house and live happily ever after!"

I took two deep breaths. *Okay, Lori, it's time to break it to her and bring out your inner truth bitch!* And this was my exact response; I saved the text 'cause I was so proud of it.

"Karen, I love you. You are one of my best friends. And I am telling you, I am coming over there to smack your face! This man is a loooooooser. You are not running to the corner store with him, much less thinking of buying some dream home, and making some new family with his bad-mannered children from his first marriage. He has no brain! I let you have your fun, and your fun has now come to an end. WE are done with him. And if you think I'm gonna let you run away with him, I'm coming to grab you and drag you back by the hair, and I will lock you in a tower myself and throw away the key!"

My friend never moved in with that man; it ended shortly after. She is finally with her real prince and living a happy life.

We now laugh at this tall tale of *big dick pixie dust*: "Remember when I almost ran away with that dumb loser and you saved me!"

Yep, I was THAT friend! The one who knew it was time to bring out the 100 percent #truthbomb. My friend actually did the rescuing of herself, I was just the one person to bring to light that she was a princess and he was the toad! Do NOT kiss the toad, ladies!

Now, these truths are not to be confused with the spilling of secrets. These honest friends are also the same ones who will get the shovel when you call and will never tell where the body is buried! They'll take that to the grave! They'll also give YOU the full truth when you need it!

Find a friend or friends, the more the merrier, to drop those truths 'cause they know you can handle it, so you can rescue your own damn self, and live sassily ever after!

To my best friend, Patti (her name will never be changed in this book to protect her identity), thank you for #truthbomb-ing me in large quantities and for sharing your tough-love facts more than I can list. I am a better person for it and love you to pieces! Love you, Patti Lewis!

Slow the Frick Down, Speedy!

....

High strung.

Hot blooded.

Busybody.

Adrenaline junkie.

In a frenzy.

Call it what you like. These are all ways in which we are moving through life too fast.

Always speeding through life's events is my middle name! I used to think it was bragging to say I was a "professional multi-tasker." I could juggle and get shit done in record time. But what I started to notice was when I was always speeding around like a race car, I was not in the present. I was always worried about what was next. I was missing what was right in front of me. In the moment. The NOW.

I was born running. My mother tells the story of how I was sprinting when I came out of the womb. I didn't sit still. Ants in my pants. To this day, I still rarely stop to take a deep breath. From a young age, I was always a busy little kid. Always doing something. And always moving quickly. Like the Energizer Bunny, I was going, going, gone! In school, I would rush to be the first person to do everything, so I could socialize and mess around. I needed to be the first one to finish every single test.

I honestly used to think I was being efficient. For most of my life, I've been a roadrunner, speeding along at record paces. I was a server at a really busy restaurant in my teens and twenties. I worked at all the top nightclubs. There was no time for breaks, no time for anything, so I would quickly grab a plate of fries and eat them as I went to the washroom. How unsanitary was that?! But it's the truth. It was either do that or don't eat. I would never once sit down to enjoy a meal. I would eat and chug water standing up. I constantly rushed. And I was always anxious. And high strung. I didn't sleep because I was used to being "on." Eating too fast has been something that's followed me my whole life. Having kids meant there was never time to eat, so I ate as quickly as possible, not chewing, not enjoying. The problem with always eating too quickly, your digestion takes a wicked turn, and you end up paying for it later with some not-so-sassy stomach issues. #TMI Speed causes anxiety, which can hit your digestion system like a brick. I was freakin' exhausted!

Technology has not been kind to us in terms of speed and moving too fast. Dial-up internet used to make us sit and wait . . . for . . . it . . . to . . . connect. Remember how long that took? Now, if it doesn't move at the speed of lightning, we lose our shit. We used to mail letters to people, then wait for a letter to be mailed back for a response. Now, we text and expect a reply within minutes. Heck, my friends will sometimes message a second time asking "You okay?" if they don't hear back from me in five minutes! Some have sent search parties if I didn't respond in record time! There is a fake urgency around everything.

But with this "hurry up to hurry up" mentality, we are missing so much of life. It's flashing before our eyes. You see, slowing the heck down requires a conscious effort. And it's tough to take the pace down a notch. But when practiced, it makes a huge difference in not only the quality of life, but in the tasks you are trying to get done.

 #storytime **Slow Movin' Stanley to the Rescue**

My great friend Stan takes his time with everything. He only focuses on one thing. It's funny because he jokes about his inability to multitask. But the thing I noticed is the task he is accomplishing is always top-notch. It's always quality over quantity. I've watched how he performs the smallest of things, and it's kind of therapeutic for us "fast-as-fuck" people to see. To see that person who just breathes through it. Chews every bite so many times it's like they can't stop enjoying all the flavors and never want the meal to end! Brushes his teeth like he is counting every stroke. He lays out his clothing before he puts it on. Has conversations with you and isn't on his gadgets (like the damn cell phones we see attached to people now, myself included). When we watch movies together, he picks up on things no one else would. His attention to the details of song lyrics and guitar chords are due to the fact he is just there, in the moment. His thoughts are on the one thing he's focused on, and it shows in the way people view him. In the work he does in his profession. In even the simplest tasks. His whole being is precise and ordered and calm. I asked him once how he did it. How did he have such intense focus and keep so slow in this very fast life?

His response was simple: "We only get one life. I choose to slow it down, or I'll be dead before I know it. I will look back and realize I only gave every person ten percent of me because my mind was ninety percent elsewhere. If I look back and see I was moving too quickly, that means I wasn't putting in the effort one hundred percent, which is what I want to put into everything I do!"

Why the heck are we in such a hurry to rush this life of ours?

Rescue your own damn self by taking on life with more of a snail's pace, putting 100 percent focus into the now, moving like Stan the Man does, and live sassily ever after!

Rapunzel

Everyone's familiar with the classic story of the kidnapped girl, Rapunzel, with magical long hair. In more recent times, Disney came out with an updated animated version called *Tangled*.

Lori's Fast and Furious Fairy Tale Breakdown:

- **Evil Witch** (because every good fairy tale has a nasty old hag) shuns a gorgeous baby to a tower hidden deep within the forest because she was destined to grow up to rule the kingdom and have amazing blonde locks!
- **Rapunzel** (chillin' in the tower) lives alone, with zero friends and no way to escape. Abolished to the forest in some penthouse prison, never to be seen again. But she loved to sing—a real Beyoncé in the making!
- **Prince Charming** is in the forest wandering (because every fairy tale has a hunky, good-looking man gallivanting happily in the greenery. It's never a sexy firefighter with a ladder, who surely could have come in handy here!).

❋ He hears her singing and asks her to let down her hair, which he uses as a rope to climb up to her room. Ever have your hair pulled? How about having a grown-ass man hanging off it? And who thinks it's a good idea to invite some random stranger into your bedroom, alone, unsupervised? Don't get me started on how this just couldn't and shouldn't happen in real life! #makesmartchoices

❋ They fall in love instantly (happens every single time in fairy tales). Who needs conversation and shared interests when there's *that* look?! #smolderingeyes

❋ The witch finds out the prince is sneaking into Rapunzel's tower. (It's kinda like when you had a boy sneaking into your room at night while your parents were sleeping!) The mean witch cuts off Rapunzel's hair, so no more booty calls from her man. Harsh! Then she banishes her into the forest and blinds the prince. Double harsh!

❋ Eventually, he hears that glorious Beyoncé voice and they reconnect like lost loves do. Her tears magically restore his sight, and they get married and move into his ten-bedroom mansion, with multiple sports cars and an in-ground pool, I mean his castle in his kingdom.

The Façade or Complete Insanity in a Nutshell:

❋ Where were the authorities? "Hi, 911, I'd like to report an emergency in the magical forest!" Wasn't anyone looking for a kidnapped little girl? This is some *America's Most Wanted* shit happening here!

❋ Stranger danger! We should never let unfamiliar peeps in our rooms just because they sweet talk us with compliments. Make smart choices, ladies! In Vegas, if you are partying with me and are part of my girl squad, no one gets left behind. I had a bestie once say, "Hey, this is John, he's having a party in his room, and I'm gonna go!" My response was this: "No, you are not going completely shit-faced drunk and alone to some random room of a potential serial killer you just met an hour ago! Give me your hand, we are grabbing a slice and heading back to our room together!" This mama bear protects her hot but tipsy little cubs.

Lori's Revamp of this Madness—*Rapunzel*, Take 2

❋ Princess lives in a tower (she can still have nice hair!).

Option #1—Girl Squad to the Rescue! I get that she was young, with no real friends, so the real-life lesson here is to get yourself a badass girl gang who has your back! If I don't get a response back from a friend to one of my texts within an hour, I'm over at her place with a search party and sniffing dogs. I like that idea that your best bitches will save you and you all climb out of that tower and head to the bar for happy hour! The "Girl Power Posse" can call the hot firemen to send that ladder to rescue their amazing friend from the tower. In having a secure feminine wolf pack, we know we can always rescue ourselves!

Option #2—Save Your Own Damn Self! Maybe she was okay sitting in sadness. The solace of silence with no one bothering her. No kids asking her, "Hey, Mom, what's there to eat?" Maybe she wanted some peace and quiet so she could calm her chaos-filled mind up in that tower away from the world. Maybe she knew how to get down with that hair of hers, but she was waiting for the timing to be right. She eventually climbs down herself, slays the crazy witch, finds a smart computer geek to marry, and they install an elevator in that tower and live a great life together!

Rescue your own damn self by believing that you don't need to find a man to rescue you at all, maybe it's you doing the rescuing or some badass babe besties, and live sassily ever after!

Don't Censor Yourself, You Sexy Mother Fucker!

If I had a dollar for every time someone told me cussing wasn't ladylike, I'd have a shit ton of fuckin' money!

I know, I know. I said I wasn't going to swear that much in this book. Call me passionate; call me uncensored. The more I try not to curse, the more curse words escape my potty mouth!

I actually didn't cuss at all for most of my life. When I first became a parent, I never dropped F-bombs. I even told my kids the words "stupid" and "shut up" were swear words. When my daughter turned fourteen, she came to me and said, "Mom, those aren't really swear words, even Hannah Montana says them!"

Hey, those words seemed rude to me, so I added them to my own list. Then I don't know what happened. Maybe I was sick of censoring myself and wanted to just be able to say whatever the fuck I wanted to say! (*Lori, such vulgar language!*)

If you have something to say, just say it! Don't censor yourself for fear of what others might think. Other people's judgments are often none of our business. It's theirs and theirs alone to deal with.

I am not just talking about swearing, though. We all should be able to speak freely without censoring or holding ourselves back. This applies to our opinions, views, and speaking our truth. Far too often, we have a comment we want to make, something we feel strongly about, information we would love to share, but we keep it to ourselves and hide out in the closet of acceptance land. We don't want to offend others, have them challenge our point of view, or worse, shun us out of the "kingdom" (*Mean Girls* mall scene, anyone?) 'cause we took the leap to go against the grain and have a differing outlook.

My motto is #nofilter. From my posts on social media to how I carry myself day-to-day, this is something I live by. That being said, my one rule is this: My opinions, views, comments, or language can't hurt anyone and have to come from a kind and loving place. Meaning, yes, there will be people who dislike swear words or might not vibe well with me when I drop the F word in every second sentence. But overall, my verbiage and the actual content and context isn't out to harm someone. It's not malicious. But if I were to "unfilter" myself and share something that might crush someone, then I do rethink how I would share that thought. I'm not talking about "offending" someone; people get their back up against the wall way too easily nowadays. #sensitivemuch If I always worried about offending people in the social media world, I would be abolished to that cold and dark tower! To me, finding something offensive often means the other person doesn't fully understand your viewpoint, or they may miss it entirely! Let's agree to disagree! We are allowed to have differing views, but society takes offense to everything and has an overly sensitive knee-jerk reaction to it all! Everyone has become overly sensitive in terms of our culture. And there is nothing I hate more than "my way or the highway" mentality, where only one viewpoint is allowed, and anyone who thinks differently might as well have a dragon breathing fire on them every minute, and fear for their life. Don't dare offend the king! Off with their heads!

Let's just start listening more when we talk about something, especially to understand the other side of our own opinions. We can all spill out our way of thinking, but leave out the cruel or harmful words. Use your voice, own it, share it, and show up like the massive queen that you are!

 #storytime   **Crystal and the Hot Body**

I met Crystal in college. She was tall and gorgeous with ebony black hair and the most beautiful body. She stood out whenever she walked into a room. But she wouldn't show off that hot bod. She always wore baggy sweats and covered up that curvy, sexy shape! You see, Crystal grew up in a house with two older sisters who weren't blessed with the same genetics. They were larger and both struggled with their weight. They had low self-esteem and often looked at Crystal with jealousy and anger, so they would belittle her, tear her down, and not allow her to be proud of her body. It became a sore spot for her that she took with her into adulthood.

I would question her all the time. "Why should their insecurities and issues impact how you dress and the confidence you have in yourself? And why should you dim your light and not shine just because they take it as an attack on their body image issues?" I would beg her to see how beautiful she was, and to own that shit!

If this is you, if this has been you, I'm asking you—fuck that! I'm telling you to let go of the maddening fear of walking into a room and having someone's opinion dictate your awesomeness. It's more on them than you. How they want to respond to anything you do, especially how you look, is their business, and it says more about them than it does you. As soon as Crystal stopped censoring herself and her body by rockin' the tight jeans and crop tops she always wanted to wear, she freed herself from being Cinderella in that locked-away dungeon! She escaped her wicked stepmother (a.k.a. her sisters' low self-esteem). She was finally free!

How many times have you stopped yourself from speaking up, saying how you feel, or sharing your ideas or input? How many times have you edited that social media post or deleted that message or picture? How many times have you pretended to be someone you aren't for fear of not being accepted for who you truly are? How many times have you had a thought or opinion you wanted to shout to the world, yet you stayed quiet?

I get it; we fear attack, ridicule, or worse, being that princess exiled to the haunted forest never to be seen again 'cause the queen looked in the mirror and was told she wasn't the prettiest in the land! The struggle is real!

Life's too short to not say "Fuck!" when you want to. Wear the clothes that make you feel bold, sexy, and goddess-like inside and out. Share your voice, your truth, and your heart when you freakin' want to!

Life moves fuckin' fast, friends! Whether you do or whether you don't, time is gonna pass anyway! So, it's time to express yourself like Madonna's hit song and own your views and opinions.

Rescue your own damn self by taking off the censor control. Stop allowing the evil queen to put you under some spell so you can't speak up. Speak loudly and unfiltered, and live sassily ever after!

Live Monotony with Excitement!

....

Life is robotic!

Life is left, right, left, right, forward march. Like a soldier, we get into this routine or system.

Yawn! Life can be boring as fuck!

We often take for granted the daily nine-to-five that seems to be on repeat. The same old partner we have to wake up next to and smell their morning breath for decades.

What if we could look at life with a different perspective?

What if we looked at all of those monotonous things with a fresh and amazing excitement?

 **#storytime   The Happy, Hungry Puppy**

I got my puppy Sam—the cutest labradoodle—a few years back. He is my world. I already had another dog, Sadie, but she was nothing like Sam. She wasn't "food obsessed." (Sam is a man after my own heart. Lori likes her food!)

You see, Sam would get so freakin' excited come feeding time, he would lose it!

Running toward the bowl of dry kibble, he would attack it

with so much excitement that he would knock it over. Kibble would be everywhere, and he would eat so quickly I swear it was in fast motion. I even had to water down his food so he would have to take his time and not eat too quickly, so he wouldn't barf it right back up.

He got so insanely happy every time I put out the kibble. It wasn't that he was starving; this boy was well fed. It was that excitement in the monotony. The life lesson I took from my little Sammy was to be excited about the day-to-day, even if it was disgusting, gross, boring kibble!

#storytime   **The Excited Dog Greeting**

If you have a dog, you know how amazing it is to be greeted by them. You could be gone a full eight-hour day or leave for two minutes, forget your keys, come back in the room, and that greeting is the same! *WOW! OMG, OMG, OMG, you're home! I love you! You are my world! I love you!* Both of my dogs greet me as if it's been forever! As if I am the most important person in their world and they are sooo excited I am in their presence. I'm not that special, but they make me feel like I am! Living life with the excitement of a dog means taking a moment to be excited about the simple and monotonous things, like seeing the same old people.

How did I apply this little "excitement" rule to life?

 **#storytime** ### Starbucks Is Monotonous, Live It Like That Excited Puppy

I go to Starbucks every single morning. It's my vice! "Venti very berry hibiscus, light ice!" I go to the same Starbucks location every day. Even when I'm on the other side of town, I will make the trek to the one I know and love. I love the baristas at MY location, and it's a part of my day I have made exciting. When I walk in, it's like that greeting my dogs give me each and every time! I get excited to see all the staff. When I make an entrance, I make them feel seen, feel special! Just like my dogs make me feel. Sure, they are the same peeps I just saw twenty-four hours prior, but I don't let that stop any amount of energy I give every time I enter! When I order my venti, I appreciate the fact I get to have it. Each day, I order it like my puppy Sam eats his kibble—with so much excitement! I mean, it's just a drink. And it's the same drink I had yesterday. But I take that moment to appreciate the sameness of it. In looking at each greeting or each Starbucks experience in a fresh new light, I live a life that can sometimes seem robotic with a little more va-va-voom!

Rescue your own damn self by being that energetic puppy or that dog filled with exploding love just living the monotony with excitement, and live sassily ever after!

Life Is About Taking a Child's Pose When You Need It!

··

Where are my fellow yogis at?

Who loves a good child's pose? Also known as balasana, for all you yoga sticklers, it's one of my favorite poses, probably because it's also called "resting pose." It's the one where you are on your knees, hip width apart, and then you sit back onto your heels. Next, you lower your torso toward your thighs. Your arms can either be along your sides resting palms up on the floor or stretched out above your head with palms facing down. Relax your neck and shoulders, then take deep, calm, and soothing breaths. Goodnight! I could legit sleep in this pose. Any good yoga class usually begins with an intro and the instructor saying, "At any point in this class if it becomes too much, or a position is just too challenging to continue, please feel more than welcome to take a soothing child's pose." There should just be a class filled with only child's pose!

Like when we hit a downward facing dog, which is really one of the hardest poses if you aren't a seasoned yogi, sign me up for the good old child's pose instead. When my day has been shit, and Warrior II isn't my jam, you will find me in—you guessed it—child's pose. I swear some classes I'm glued in this resting pose, and it just feels like a complete AHH!

Child's pose helps reduce stress, anxiety, and fatigue. If only I could bottle this up and sell it, I'd be rich!

But wait, maybe in life we can just take more child's poses.

When we are feeling too anxious, stressed, tired, lost, at our wits' end, unclear, unsure, like losing your shit is just around the corner, like you might burst any second, insert child's pose!

Now you aren't gonna drop to your hands and knees on the floor in Costco (although if you did, I wouldn't judge you for it!). But let's apply this concept to life and create our own versions of balasana.

Child's pose for love, Take 1

Relationships are freakin' hard! What if when we are feeling *enough is enough* in our marriage or love affair, we could take a child's pose? A break, just like Ross and Rachel did on *Friends*. What if these mini rests or breaks could help us soul search, reset, think about what we really want and need, and then return clearer and less stressed? Heck, once you are in your child's pose of a relationship break and on Tinder for a while, you're sure to come racing back. Look at what happened to Ross and Rachel—they got back together (epic writing fail IMO, #teamjoey all the way!).

The mom's child's pose, *Take 2*

"1, 2, 3, 4, 5, 6, 7 . . . sorry, hold up, 8, 9, 10." That was me, standing in a closet or in the master en suite or on the other side of the door away from my kids, counting to freakin' ten! Moms, ya feel me? Show of hands, who knows what it's like to need to take a child's pose from motherhood? *Ew, I don't want that for dinner; Mom, where's my ___?; Mom, can you ___?; Mom, I need a ride to ___; Mom, I hate you!; Mom, I don't want to___!; Mom, Mom, hey, Mom!*

Yeah, count to one hundred on this one if you need it! I remember once my toddler wouldn't get dressed. I was so ready to lose my cool, and instead I went on the front porch (leaving her safe inside), and started my child's pose: 1, 2, 3, 4 . . . And at 10, I could feel my face stop being so red it was going to burst off my head. I took one more breath and headed back inside to begin the negotiations with my three-year-old on the importance of wearing pants in the winter. That was my resting pose break, my moment to lower my anxiety, stress, and just breathe. Reset! So, I could then take on the more challenging poses (in yoga) or times (in life).

This same rule can be used for all the moms of teens. Y'all have a special place in my heart. Where are my moms of hormonal teenage girls at? Let's take a moment of silence to remember our lost sanity. Parenting a teenage girl warrants us parents a special place in Heaven, I think, with unlimited wine, Botox from the wrinkles they give us, and all-round gold star status.

My teenager makes me need child's pose, Take 3

My daughter is now nineteen; how she made it to this age, I will never know! My sanity and patience were pushed to the brink of madness, but my ability to ensure I took a child's pose on multiple occasions is what ensured her life-span to be longer. Now, I was once a teenage girl, so my mother would say I got what I deserved.

My daughter was a door slammer. Whenever she was upset, she rushed quickly like an escaped convict to her room and SLAM! When she hated that she couldn't go out with her friends till 1 a.m., she'd run to her room and SLAM! Little brother was bothering her, SLAM! See the theme here?

One day, the slamming had worn on me. I had asked her to do something (probably something torturous, like emptying the dishwasher or folding some laundry . . . 'cause how dare I ask my own child to help around the house in which she lives rent free!). Insert the mad dash to her room, and SLAM! 1, 2, 3, 4, 5 . . . yep, I was gonna pull out the toddler parent methodology . . . 6, 7 . . . SLAM! Wait, what?! The counting I was trying to do to take my child's pose didn't work. I hadn't reacted to the first slam, and *did she, wait, did she just slam it again, to get a reaction from me?! Breathe, Lori! Deep breaths! Take your child's pose. 8, 9* . . . SLAM! OH, HELL NO!

Insert Mom doing the mad dash to her daughter's room. I opened her door and screamed, "I invented that slam, girl, you don't get to use that slam on me, I'm the slam-freakin'-master! I am the queen of the tantrums. The head bitch of the badass stompers! Do not slam your door again!" Whew, there I was, a mom in control. As I closed her door softly behind me and walked away, I was so glad I resolved that! And SLAM! She actually opened her door behind me, then slammed it again! Now, I'm both proud and not proud of my next action. I turned around, karate kicked her door with my bare foot (Moms have super-human powers in situations when needed), and the door busted off the doorframe. (I am not promoting this level of hostility, I'm just saying, no judgments. I was at my wits' end that day.) Her eyes widened. "There, now your door isn't on the frame, so you CAN'T SLAM IT!"

Now, the door kick wasn't the child's pose I should have dropped into before taking the door-kicking action (again, proud but also not proud, when ya know, ya know!). I grabbed the keys to my car and left the house to go for a little drive with AC/DC blasting for ten minutes. I called my bestie once I parked down the street for a few minutes so I could bitch about my teenage daughter being taken over by a door-slamming alien. This was my child's pose. My bestie, Patti, reminded me that she felt zero sympathy for me since she had not one but two of those little monsters to deal with. The moral of the story is, parents, you need to reinvent what your rest, reset, calm, child's pose will look like as those little beasts grow up!

I could go on and on about how a child's pose can be used in life. For teens heading from high school to college or university, this could be a "gap year," where they want a break to soul search and decide what they wanna be when they grow up. Heck, even I still don't know at forty-five!

Hell, your resting pose could be a girls' weekend away. OMG, do I ever need Vegas with my besties to be a resting pose! It's a time to lower anxiety, stress, regroup, then come back when you are ready with Pinot Grigio pulsing through your veins. Can I get an "AMEN" and a mimosa at 6 a.m. in the airport? I'm ready to party!

Your child's pose is your moment to regroup. Mine just happens to need slutty outfits, dancing till 1 a.m., and making terrible choices!

Attention, class of life, if at any time it becomes too much, too strenuous, too stressful, too WTF, I invite you to rescue your own damn self by taking a child's pose, and live sassily ever after!

Dirty Dancing

Nobody puts Baby in a corner.

–Johnny Castle

If you haven't seen this movie, you are dead to me! Legit! Stop reading. Put down the book. Open up the old Netflix app on the TV, scroll to find it, and watch. I'll wait here for you. Your life is about to change in a matter of an hour and forty-five minutes! Report back to me when Johnny and Baby warm your heart!

My favorite line from the whole movie: "I'm doing this to save your ass, but what I really wanna do is drop you on it!" Ladies, ya feel me? I can think of many men I would have liked to have used this statement on! #truestory

Here's the rundown:

- Daddy's rich little good girl (Frances, a.k.a. Baby) goes away for the summer with her family.
- She meets a hot, sexy, freakin' amazing bad boy, dancing-machine stud (Johnny). RIP, Patrick Swayze. (This movie can never be redone because no one is like him!)
- He teaches her to dance, they fall in love, but it's not allowed (good girl, bad boy—you know the drill!).

- He gets fired and has to miss the big year-end celebration, normally done with some kick-ass dance finale!
- But just at the last moment, he storms into that rec hall, saves her from the corner she's in, they dance their asses off, and live happily ever after!

Okay, listen, we all have that one love. That amazing summer fling. That "hottest sex ever" guy! The love that was so intense but never lasts. We have all fallen for that guy who looks terrible on paper, but his ass looks amazing in tight jeans, and he has a stellar smile.

This movie never had a sequel, but I think it's safe to say we all knew they actually didn't leave the resort, get married, open a dance studio, have two kids and a dog, and live happily ever after!

Before I rewrote this ending, I had a thought. What if being in the corner isn't so bad? Maybe we need that "time out" to regroup. Time to take a deep breath, calm the frick down, focus, recharge, count to ten, then come bursting out of the damn corner ourselves with a new zest for life!

When life slaps us in the face or makes us stop and struggle, maybe we need that little corner to think of our own solutions and absorb them. Then make our comeback outta the damn despair, a.k.a. the corner!

Back to the rewrite. Here is my ending . . . and it's a goodie!

I won't cut the dance scene, 'cause let's be honest, we've all done that scene while in our bedrooms or living rooms whenever "The Time of My Life" comes on the radio. Or crawled on our hands and knees singing "Lover Boy." Y'all know you have done it too! Guilty as charged!

So, let the epic dance scene happen, especially because we would never say no to Patrick Swayze in a black tank top, mmm, wait, where was I? Oh right, dance, then I see Baby ditching that hot babe Johnny and taking on the world. Johnny didn't save her after all, he just did that dirty mambo with her. Proved the point of fighting for equality. For race. Sex. Class. I hardly think that resort really changed their mentality because of Johnny and Baby's epic dance ending. Look at the state of the world even now!

I'm saying maybe Baby would have come out of the corner herself and danced her ass off. Did Johnny rescue her? Nope. He was her summer love. Short term. Hot sex. Good kisser!

I think she came out of the corner to dance and prove a point. Then she became an amazing human rights advocate and saved the world. A game-changing lawyer or even a big-name Supreme Court judge.

Nobody puts Lori in a corner. Legit, I remind myself of this concept almost daily, especially when I'm in my "time out" or have my back pressed up against a wall from this insanity called life.

I feel like we all get backed into corners.

We all get tired.

We all fall into ruts.

We all have moments of despair, like we just can't do it anymore.

We are often told *no* or *you can't*. Sometimes, we are about to lose our shit and just don't have the answers.

What matters most is what we do in those moments, who we are, how we choose to show up, how we choose to evolve, rise, and grow from it. Make sure you do a super cheeky dance with a hot Swayze-like sexpot, THEN take on the world!

So, take your little corner moment to regroup, then rescue your own damn self, and live sassily ever after!

Being Naked Rules!

Picture this: You're showering in a communal area at the gym, baring it all. Uninhibited under the water, of course. Once done, you quickly wrap a towel around yourself and scurry toward the change room area to get dressed, hoping no one sees you. That fear someone might sneak a peek as you disrobe to get your clothes on. But why? Why are we so scared of others looking at us in the buff? I mean, don't we all have the kibbles and bits, parts and pieces? Last I checked, we all had vaginas and boobs (and men have penises! *Kindergarten Cop*, anyone?). When did it become so scary to just be in the flesh around others?

Wanna know a secret? Lean in closer . . . I wasn't always THIS confident! Gasp! I know, right? I had to work for it. You see, once upon a time there was a girl who was not comfortable being naked at all.

I was in Las Vegas at Caesars Palace about nine years ago, in their amazing hydrotherapy spa. It's a little piece of heaven outfitted with a dry sauna, a steam room, and even a room that snows on you and is next level freezing-your-nipples-off kinda cold! Sign me up for that! It has hot tubs, plunge pools, and so much more. It's the shit! I went the first day and was super covered up. I saw that clothing was "optional," but the space was only for women, not co-ed. Still, I would wrap my towel around myself everywhere I went, which meant I wasn't fully experiencing it all since I was so hung up on my body (which was at the time ultra-lean and amazing). I went back on day two and there was a large group of European ladies in their fifties. They saw me scurry from room to room with my tightly wrapped towel. We were all in the sauna together at one point, and one very nice buck-naked woman watched as I carefully kept myself mummy-like from head to toe. In her beautiful Italian accent, she said, "My darling, if I had a body like yours, I would be walking around the casino and Vegas strip with no clothes on. Get naked, bella!"

She was telling me to stop the madness, so I actually let the towel drop. And I swear, at that moment I felt like I could take on the world. I remember sitting and chatting with them about the female body and how Europeans view it so much differently. Nudity isn't as sexual; it's more just a way of life to embrace your body and feel at home in your skin. These women were so much more comfortable with their naked selves, regardless of their body shape and their fat percentage. Unlike in North America, in Europe, women have more confidence being naked. They aren't so attached to their size or perfection, and body ideals just aren't as much of a "thing." They feel so body-free. I've tried to take that experience of being naked at the Palace with me even almost a decade later. I will go topless at the hotel pool and not give a crap (if it is a topless pool, that is—let's look for signs, my friends, that could be dangerous!).

But I didn't embrace my nakedness right away. It took me more time and more experiences to simply let it all hang out. Literally and figuratively!

I was in Italy traveling with Tina, a client and a friend, about seven years ago. We stayed in a cute little apartment when we were there. She was super comfortable being naked, and because she was doing a fitness competition, she was lean and amazing! I wasn't as lean, but I felt super comfortable as both of us were having our own naked party. As soon as we'd get back to our hotel room, it was clothes off, let it all hang out! We would do everything naked: eat, sleep, just lounge and relax, and simply be. In our full glory. Stripped nude. I realized we were both just shells, physical bodies. It felt so empowering to walk about freely, au naturel. It felt good to not be so focused on the size of my ass, if I was lean enough, or if it was okay that I wasn't the same size as her. In the end, after doing it over and over, I forgot about the nonsense that can sometimes fill my head and just did it. Practice makes perfect with this one. I can assure you that the more you just do it, the more you can own the shit out of the skin you're in!

Babes, peeps, future fellow nudists, I will tell you . . .

Once you learn to bare it all and let the vagina and nips breathe free, you will rescue your own damn self, and live sassily ever after!

Have Empathy in Healthy Amounts or End Up Like John Coffey

....

I am one of the most empathetic people on the planet. "I see dead people!" (*The Sixth Sense*, anyone?) No, not that. I "feel" what other people are feeling, even if it might not be something affecting me directly or something I have experienced myself. I've always been that person who reads the room, absorbs the energy or aura, gets right into people's souls. I have had this my whole life. Like a sponge, I absorb all the emotions, feelings, and just all the things around me. I know when someone is off; I see it in their eyes, I hear it in their voice, and it almost stabs me in the heart. It's so piercing to me! The world around us. People around us.

Growing up, my mother wasn't empathetic at all. Her upbringing impacted what she takes on in terms of energy fields. But my dad, wow, he is a feeler! During my preteen years, I would see the emotion in his six-foot-two-inch frame. He would have tears in his eyes just watching the news sometimes. And when one of the news anchors retired, he cried for him.

"Dad, did you even know this guy in real life, or is it just from watching him read the news for twenty-five years?"

But my dad absorbed the emotions from the news anchor as

he read those final goodbyes and sobbed. My dad saw in his eyes how upsetting it must be to know that he was reading for the final time and leaving his passion. My dad felt it. Heck, he even cried at some commercials!

Like him, I feel hard too. I experience everything other people go through. Some say I'm psychic (or do they mean psycho?), but I am that girl who senses when someone is going through something and will send them a random text out of the blue: "Hi. Thinking of you. Here if you need me!"

The Green Mile is one of my favorite movies!

John Coffey is a tall drink of a big man. His character felt the pain of other people, so much so he would try to take that pain from them, suck it out of them, and try to save them. To the point of exhaustion. It sucked HIS energy out, to rescue them. Mr. Jangles was a little mouse, who was trampled, but John resuscitated the mouse back to life (yes, pure CPR style, ew!). How awesome is that?!

That is me—I am John Coffey. I see a local business struggling, and I need to save it. I see someone crying from a heartbreak, and I need to fix them and make them happy again. That person is struggling—I can feel the intensity of their searing pain inside of me. It's a great trait to have, but it's also one that is super draining.

Spoiler alert: Skip over this next part if you haven't seen the end of *The Green Mile*.

After trying so hard to help people, heal people, be the most empathic man ever, John Coffey is put to death. It reminded me that while empathy in small amounts is good, too much of a good thing turns bad!

I struggled with severe anxiety for a while, the bulk of taking on everyone else's problems and absorbing their emotions became detrimental to my own health and well-being.

In the movie, John talks about being a lonely robin, being tired, alone, seeing people being ugly to one another. He's tired of not being able to help everyone. Tired of being in so much pain. John speaks of wanting to end it, and he would if he could. Gasp! Wow, that shows how much damage an overly empathic person could do to themselves if they don't get a handle on the pressure level before they burst. We have to remember to always put ourselves first. Yep, oxygen mask analogy here. You cannot save anyone unless you yourself are alive and breathing. And not being burned alive by anxiety inside, like I was, or put to death, like John Coffey.

Turn off the news if you need to. Or take that much-needed social media detox. Sometimes, the weight of what's happening outside of us is just too much. And remember that our children are watching us, too, and might end up being empathic little spirits who feel just as hard.

The fixers.

The healers.

The solvers.

Let's give small doses of our time and energy, but remember you can't be in every place, every time, fixing everyone. You will explode or burn trying. Feel for the person, but don't give all of your oxygen to them. In having empathy for others, we don't want to lose ourselves in the process.

Rescue your own damn self by keeping healthy levels of empathy, 'cause it can really be a good thing in moderation, and live sassily ever after!

Life Is Like a Starbucks Drink: Fully Customizable!

....

I really should think about asking Starbucks to sponsor me and my book. I mean, I think I mention them about twenty times.

Starbucks is life! It's a fact! Wait, that's not the point of this lesson.

Who here enjoys Starbucks as much as I do? I am a Starbucks snob! I have it each and every day, and I've had it for years. I am not a nice person without it! It's my vice, my thing, my routine.

Those who are Starbucks lovers know that just because the menu lists what it lists, it doesn't mean you can't ask for what you want.

Just because it says "Mocha Frappuccino," doesn't mean that's what you have to order. "I'll have a grande mocha frappé in a venti cup, extra ice, blend for ten more seconds, hold the whip, extra three pumps of mocha, caramel layer with chocolate drizzle, and top it with cookie crumble. Oh, and please ensure it's to a temp of ten degrees! Name is Victoria!"

I swear you need a Bachelor of Social Work with a master's degree in patience to serve customers and work as a barista at Starbucks! We don't give the staff enough credit for the madness that prevails and continues to get more out of control!

#truthbomb: Life is like that Starbucks drink: it's what you want, what you make it, what you create, and fully customizable!

You don't have to live life with what's on the menu. Create your own damn drink, a.k.a. life!

Want to live bigger? Order a trenta and live your life LARGE! (For the Starbucks newbies, this is a large, made larger, then made even larger—it's giant!)

Feeling sweet and sassy—get an iced mocha latte to cool yourself down!

And just like if they mess up that Starbucks drink of yours, you can send it back and they'll fix it for you. They'll make it right!

In life, we can fuck things up, then fix them! Remake the drink, redo, and try again!

Heck, some new Starbucks drink creations are a hit, and some are an epic miss and taste like shit! We can change our minds and try something new any time, and hello, the same applies to life!

This is North America in the year 2021, so unless you come from a family of arranged marriages, you are the one who gets to pick your partner. YOU can choose to be married—or not! "I'll take one Channing Tatum to go, please! Wrap it up!"

Want kids? I'll take two, "with extra whip!" In society, it's also now common to choose not to have them. Life is your customization!

Lawyers, doctors, firefighters, not anymore! Careers now are a "follow your passion" and a "think outside the box" kinda choice! Customizable! You almost get to create your dream career! Gone are the nine-to-five hours at the same company for life. Go to college or university, learn online, work online, make up your own business idea, launch a product or invention, carve out your own career path. The sky's the limit now in terms of how we can choose to work and earn money.

Don't like the location where you're living? Sell everything and move across the country. Customize where you wake up every day, and where you go to bed. When that location gets tiring, move again.

Relationships aren't just boy/girl anymore. Years ago when Ellen came out on her sitcom, audiences gasped. Now, there wouldn't be a peep. LGBTQIA2+ isn't so "different" or "shocking." There are no more set rules for who you choose to have sex with or to not have sex with! Love who you love. No one cares anymore! You do you, boo!

Dye your hair or shave your head. Get a tattoo or two and piercings, and work in finance, not just in tattoo shops. No one judges anymore! I have purple and magenta hair, and no one bats an eyelash at my kid's soccer games. We get to choose!

Life is about choices. Just like that Starbucks drink. The varieties are endless. It's what YOU make it!

Rescue your own damn self by customizing your own damn life just how you want it, and live sassily ever after!

The Princess and the Frog

Disney put their updated spin on the story of a prince who has been turned into a frog by an evil witch doctor and the beautiful woman who tries to free him by making out with him. Because of this tale, we've grown up thinking we need to kiss a lot of frogs (a.k.a. duds) before we find our prince (a.k.a. true love).

Lori's Fast and Furious Fairy Tale Breakdown:

* The (future) princess is **Tiana**, a beauty who needs money to open her dream restaurant and is desperate enough to kiss a frog to get it. Ew!
* The **Frog** is actually a real prince who is under a spell by, you guessed it, a wicked witch doctor, who has his own devious plans to steal the royal riches.
* Because Tiana isn't a princess, by kissing the frog prince, she, too, is turned into a frog. Ew and ew! (Can you tell I think frogs are gross?!) The two hop away and hide out in a swamp where they befriend other animals (naturally) and fall in love (of course) while trying to plan their future.

* A voodoo queen reverses the curse, the frog lovers are returned to their human forms, Tiana is turned into a princess, and the happy couple marry and open a trendy restaurant.

The Facade or Complete Insanity in a Nutshell:

* Who the heck believes that a frog is really a cursed prince? Don't kiss amphibians! And don't believe it when a guy says he's really something else. Remember those fake online dating profiles?!
* Why is it that we always have to be searching for the rich, powerful prince to help us live a life of bliss? In every fairy tale, it's always a woman's desperate need for a prince's love or money to make her dreams come true. It's never the guy who makes a decent living in the kingdom owning the shoe repair shop. We're always aiming high, and it's always about looks and riches! Why not the guy with a great personality, average looks, and job security?!

Lori's Revamp of this Madness—*The Princess and the Dog* (no, that's not a spelling mistake, I want it to be a dog, not a frog!), Take 2

I kiss my dog all the time, and I don't want him to turn into some annoying human! I like my dog because he's a dog! Maybe I've had so much relationship trauma from searching for my own prince that I just want a fluffy old, reliable dog, and I will save up the funds for my new business venture myself!

Maybe if I kiss my dog/frog, he will stay a dog/frog, and I won't become his princess. I have clients and friends who have chosen a life of being single. They have cats, dogs, and various pets for company and comfort. My one friend Jenny bought her own house, started her own hair salon, has two dogs and a cat, and never wants to get married. She dates, but then they go home to their kingdoms and she stays in hers! She rules her domain, and they rule theirs!

Let's all stop believing that ugly frog needs to turn into some hot stud muffin prince to save us.

Rescue your own damn self by staying away from slimy frogs asking to be kissed, and live sassily ever after!

Fitness Doesn't Have to Be So Fuckin' Complex!

....

I have been a fitness coach, personal trainer, avid lifter, and worker-outer for thirty years!

When I was writing this book, I started out thinking it would have tons of chapters about all the life lessons I learned being in the crazy fitness industry. I assumed it would have so many witty tips on how to reach your lofty goals and live a life filled with rock-hard abs and a tight ass to go with it!

But as I continued writing, I realized **I only learned one real lesson about fitness.**

Fitness (which can include a broad scope of things like workouts and nutrition) doesn't have to be so fuckin' complicated or complex!

The industry makes it that way. The bullshit we have been told, then untold for centuries is complete and utter nonsense.

It's a trillion-dollar industry that just wants to keep us guessing, thinking, overthinking, rethinking, then losing our minds trying to figure it out.

A world where they want us never reaching our goals, never feeling good in our bodies, or feeling truly confident in our skin.

They want us to always be on the hunt for the new magic workout, cutting-edge pill or drink, or latest craze in terms of a fad diet promising some overnight transformation.

They want us to find short-term success with complicated strategies that we can't sustain. It's a vicious cycle and much like a drug addict continues to need their next "fix," we continue to go for the dopamine hit every single time. The yo-yo diets, the extreme diets, the waist-trainers, the fat-melt-away creams, the thighmasters, or other insane workout contraptions.

I think about the number of years, decades really, I have spent trying to figure out some complex scientific approach or which "diet craze" really is the one to prescribe to my clients that works for life.

Come a little closer, I need to whisper this little tidbit of secret intel I have . . . IT DOESN'T FREAKIN' EXIST! (You thought I was going to say the other F word there, didn't ya? Yeah, IT DOESN'T FUCKIN' EXIST EITHER!)

The secret to finding that sweet spot of sustainable fitness and body goals, and results for life, is to stop making it so damn hard! Dumb it the heck down and save yourself from the madness of locking yourself away in some tower with no carbs. Or thinking that adding more cardio or more deprivation is going to help you live happily ever after.

I don't even want to spend tons of time on this subject because

I don't think fitness tells us anything in terms of life. Live your life and stop worrying so much about your body—it will find its way to where it needs to be.

Here are my subplots to simplifying things for yourself:

Plot #1—Weight train or remain the same

Lift weights, or your toddler if you don't have access to dumb-bells, three times a week. Don't overtrain, but lift some freakin' weights! Results for life are gonna happen when you stop living on a treadmill like a cardio crack addict junkie and hit the armor!

Plot #2—Cardio sucks ass

I am the most passionate about this one. Cardio is like Superman's *kryptonite*. It makes you lose lean muscle and become a meek and weak version of yourself. And the industry feeds the nonsense to us that more, more, more is better. Stop the madness. Sure, if you love running, run, but remember it is not the top tool to pick for any type of physique transformation.

Plot #3—Stop trying to cut shit out for nutrition

Instead of saying "eat this, not that" or "good versus bad" or "clean versus dirty," try to nourish your body with food you love. Eat more green shit, add more protein. If you like plant-based items or have vegan beliefs, go for it, but don't jump on that train just because it's the latest trend. If you like meat, eat it. Just don't start eating "carnivore" 'cause Joe Rogan says so on his podcast! (Disclaimer: I love Joe Rogan and will speak no ill against him, but most people, especially men, seem to jump aboard whatever trend he's on.) My point is, whatever you choose to eat, do so because you want to, not because you have to. Do it because it makes you feel incredible inside and out.

Plot #4—What works for one doesn't work for the rest and might not work forever

Remember, as we age our bodies shift, and hormonally, we change. Listen to your body and continue to always make choices for everything you do based on the internal. Focus on **feeling better**, and in the end, you will end up **looking better! When you feel good, you look good!**

I could throw in thousands of clients' stories from my career, where they followed my guidance and are looking hot AF and owning it! But really, we have bigger shit to worry about in life. Fitness is such a small part of the very amazing human beings that we are. Our body is a vessel; we need to stop focusing so much on changing it, molding it, trimming it away, losing weight, getting smaller, being leaner, and thinking that our "external shell" is so damn important! Sure, it can be a focus. I get it; we want to look good in those skinny jeans and have a nice ass, but let's make it less about extremes, madness, or insanity.

Simple solutions aren't sexy, so they don't sell or make the big bucks, but they work! Wrapping a big bow around something to make it look more complex doesn't mean it's the best way. Dumb it down. Simple is easier and works!

Rescue your own damn self by keeping fitness simple, fun, and less of a focus, and live sassily ever after!

GPS the Shit Out of Life and Find Your Own Damn Way!

What if I told you we all have our own inner guidance system that can help us get from here to where we want to go in life? Like finding your own roadside adventure in that super cool Barbie Dream Car.

Your inner GPS, a.k.a. your "roadmap," is telling you how to get from point A to B.

All you need to do is figure out where you want to go, then lock down getting there by goal setting, game planning, visualizing, and pulling up your big girl panties and taking action!

The problem is that most of us don't get out of our own damn way. We start our engines, then sit idle while contemplating even leaving the garage. When we hit a bumpy road or that scary dead end, we just give up. Slam the breaks, park the car, and call an Uber!

Wrong turns and detours cause us to stress and panic, and we can't accept that maybe it's taking us in the same direction of our final destination on a more scenic route.

If you could see your perfect life, what would it look like? Don't let anyone else tell you what this is, don't let judgments get in the way—spill it! What's your ultimate vision?

You see, no one ever really asks us this. We are told how life should look. How our whole cycle of growing and aging is supposed to play out. THEY tell us how it's gonna be.

Step one: Be born, grow up.

Step two: Fall in love, get married.

Step three: Fend off questions about babies five minutes into the wedding.

Step four: Fend off questions about baby number two when baby number one is literally crowning out of your vagina. Not kidding, this happens!

Step five: Juggle being a kick-ass mom and returning to an amazing career as fast as possible, while keeping a super clean house, amazing meals on the table, and your body near perfection for social media. Of course, your marriage is meant to be solid despite neglecting one another and being barely unable to keep your shit together behind closed doors.

What if that was never your dream but one stuffed down your throat from your youth?

What if you just took this path 'cause that's the only way you thought you could go?

My friend Dani made a decision to not have kids. Gasp! She decided to focus on her amazing career, not get married, and her Italian mama is still cringing about it. But she wrote her own roadmap early in life and knew exactly where she wanted it to take her for her adventure. Sure, there were detours in her profession, job changes, losses, moves to different cities, but she knew what her main point forms looked like, beyond the nonsense we are fed by society. She listened to her inner voice, her GPS, and found her ultimate destination. Dani was invigorated by her career and climbing up the giant corporate ladders while she kept her eye on the prize!

 #storytime **The Dead End . . . What the Frick Now?!**

Sometimes in life, we are GPSing the shit out of it when we hit a dead end. I invite you to do what my friend Alyssa did.

Alyssa had the ultimate life. The perfect house. The perfect dogs. The perfect partner. Until one day, she realized she had nothing of her own. He picked the house, he picked the dogs, and he wasn't so damn perfect after all. One day, she just hit that wall. She couldn't do it anymore.

She didn't back up (insert annoying beeping sound for big trucks backing up!). Sure, she could have put it into reverse and returned to the madness that was behind her. The house she didn't like, the partner who wasn't what she truly wanted.

But she saw that wall, and she went one hundred and twenty miles per hour right fuckin' through it! She packed her bags and moved to Europe with nothing. No dogs, no house, and no partner. She got a wicked job over there, met an amazing man, and rescued a sweet dog from the streets!

She didn't let the wall (her dead end) stop her—and don't let your dead end stop you!

Rescue your own damn self by writing your own directions or map of adventures, and live sassily ever after!

Stop Comparing Strawberries to Raspberries: Both Are Sweet!

Let's talk about the "comparison game."

That mental mind fuck we all do when we see an inspiring physique. Or a "pro." Or a "celeb." Or an "influencer."

I get it; we scroll the 'gram. We see the pics. We think, *Wow. I wanna look like her.*

But I'm gonna let you in on a little secret . . . You can only be YOUR best. You can't turn into someone else. Gasp!

You can't compare strawberries to raspberries. Both are delicious. But different.

As a fitness coach, I have clients constantly sending me pics of their favorite pro competitors or fitness models or influencers on the old 'gram. "I want to look like her. What do I have to do to look like that girl?"

My life lesson is this: **Stop fuckin' trying to be like someone else!**

I once did a side-by-side picture comparison of myself and this top bikini pro who has been winning shows and is all over the internet. We'll call her "Stacey." I took our two pics, hers on the left, and mine on the right. We are both five foot eight. Tall, beautiful goddesses! Booyah! We are the same weight. Her last stage weight was the exact weight I was for my last photoshoot and the weight that I continue to maintain. Those are the only two things we share. The pics show that although we were the same height and weight, I was larger, I was fuller. The two bodies didn't look the same. We are very different structures. I will never ever look like her. And #truthbomb: I don't want to!

Stacey, the bikini pro:
- Twenty-three years old.
- A fitness model with paid sponsorships (her body literally pays her bills).
- No kids.
- IFBB pro bikini competitor who lives for her workouts. The ultra-lean body is needed year-round, as it's her bread and butter.
- Lives. Breathes. Competes. And in that world 24/7, 365!
- She has the big G: Genetics. Born with the tiniest waist on the planet, rumored to be only twenty-one inches.
- She has a personal trainer at a killer gym. And she is able to push herself to 200 percent for all of her workouts.
- Her meals are timed and planned year-round.
- She does cardio. Lots of it!
- Her boyfriend also lives the lifestyle of being an IFBB pro bodybuilder. It's his life, income, and world as well.

- X lbs. (not putting weight for fear others will compare). Same weight as me, but harder. Leaner. More muscle in the booty.
- Did I mention she was twenty-freakin'-three years old?

Lori, the "not" bikini pro:
- Forty-five years old.
- An empowerment and life coach, and author.
- Two kids, teenagers (fifteen and nineteen).
- Sure, I once lived the life of a competitor. But my body has nothing to do with my talent as a coach. No one cares how I look. Competing and the gym are not my world. And disclaimer: Wine is my friend!
- The G word again: Genetics. I was also born with a small waist-to-hip ratio but not as blessed as Stacey and her anomaly of a tiny little waist! Mine is about twenty-five inches at its smallest.
- I work out at home by myself with minimal equipment. Most of my workout you will find me laying on the floor frog pumping and scrolling the 'gram.
- I eat whatever. Whenever. No macros. No structure. No real counting or planning.
- No cardio. Just dog walks.
- My family and friends couldn't care less about fitness and bodybuilding.

- X lbs., same weight as bikini pro, but I'm softer. I lost forty pounds in the last year, so it takes time to tighten and harden. Even though our numbers are the same, the density is very different. My glutes are a work in progress.
- I am old(er)! Hormonal shifts. Perimenopause, and menopause around the horizon, means internal shit is happening beyond my control. It's called aging, and it's a thing. I also have hypothyroidism. Not sure about her. But that's my story. Gravity also takes over as we age. So shit doesn't sit as high and tight as it once did.

Strawberries and raspberries, friends! Can't compare!

I'm a huge fan of Stacey, and honestly, I would never tear down any person for how they choose to look or where they choose to put their focus, so this isn't a diss on her at all. Bravo! And to be her age and have such amazing gifts and talents. Go get it, girl!

We all have choices, directions, and where we choose to focus our energy. I don't fault her for having her body as the top tier of her life. That's her choice. I would be doing the same thing if I had her age and genetics. Hell yeah!

I'm not saying either way is better. I enjoy all types of berries! Here's what I learned to help us appreciate our unique bodies and gifts:

- You can only be *your* best you. Stop comparing yourself with anyone else.

- Weight doesn't mean anything. You can weigh the same, and it can look and feel different on each individual.

- We choose what is our focus, our life, our time spent. So, if you always compare yourself to someone else, it means you have to have the same everything as them!

- Both of our bodies are amazing. Lean and strong. No one gets to say what is "better." They are different. And that's what makes the world a beautiful place.

- You don't know what goes on behind the scenes for someone to look the way they do. And don't believe everything you see on the 'gram.

- Be inspired by others but stop trying to BE others. And inspire others by focusing on being YOUR best.

Rescue your own damn self by being the best fruit you can be and by not trying to be a blueberry if you are a blackberry, or a peach if you are a mango, and live sassily ever after!

50 First Dates

My name is Lori, and I will watch any romantic comedy starring Drew Barrymore and Adam Sandler sixty-five billion times! This epic romantic comedy is my favorite. It's tied to this little space in my heart, and I just can't get enough of it.

Recap for those who can't remember it (lol):

- Lucy (Drew Barrymore) is in a car accident leaving her with no short-term memory; she can't remember anything past the day of the accident. Every single day she wakes up and doesn't remember a damn thing!
- Henry (Adam Sandler) sees her in a café and falls for her instantly, but when he realizes she has no memory of him, he has to "win her over" every single day!
- Deep down she really does fall for him and remembers him as she sings "Wouldn't It Be Nice." But to live happily ever after, he's got to remind her every single day with a video of who he is, why she fell in love with him, and why they are living this fairy tale with a happy ending!

Pass the tissues! This movie has me sobbing every single time! And it's not even sad!

I actually don't want to rewrite this romantic comedy—I wanna take a lesson from it.

Forgetting everything that happens the days, weeks, or months prior might not be such a bad thing. I understand the seriousness of amnesia, and this isn't meant to minimize anyone who has ever had a loved one navigate any form of memory loss.

Stay with me on this one, I have a point.

In love, what if every single day we woke up and the person who has our heart had to prove themselves worthy. Imagine if the person of our dreams had to spend each and every new day reminding us of why we are smitten with them, why we chose them, and why we should keep choosing them!

Any baggage or upset from the day before can be left where it belongs, in the past. Forgetting about it and getting over it. Starting each new day fresh and free of the bad memories that didn't serve us. Every day is a fresh new start.

Imagine waking up not knowing what the day will bring. Not harboring regrets. Not hanging onto past sadness or negative vibes.

I love the thought of needing to do this to prove to my love that he chose me for a reason and reminding him every day of why. Sobbing again here! That's romance!

So, maybe we all need to take a page from *50 First Dates* and start new days with a clean slate. A new beginning with every sunrise to show everyone around us that we are the one they need to give the rose to at the rose ceremony! (*The Bachelor*, anyone?)

Rescue your own damn self by forgetting a little, forgiving a little, reminding a little, and earning that love every damn day, and live sassily ever after!

Your Vagina Is a Wonderland!

Front Bottom.

Lady Parts.

C*nt. (I refuse to say or even type this word! You know the one!) #thecwordistillcantsay

P*ssy. (Again, I need to censor this one, not sure why, but this word is a swear word to me.)

Twat.

Box.

Honeypot.

Beaver.

Muff.

Pum-Pum.

Love Box.

Jelly Roll.

Genitalia.

Call it what you want to, I am talking about the Va-jay-jay. The VAGINA!

 **The Ugly Vagina**

This story is not mine. It was one told to me by my client Melissa and her daughter Heidi. Names have been changed out of respect for their privacy. This story is one that to this day I still laugh about, but I can also relate to that feeling because I, too, had an "ugly vagina!"

Melissa and I were chatting in one of our training sessions and she said, "I was sleeping soundly last night at ten when my door burst open and my seventeen-year-old daughter, Heidi, threw herself on my bed in a complete fluster. She was crying. 'I think something is wrong with me!' I was totally startled and tried to process what the heck was happening while being happy it wasn't some serial killer attacking me in my sleep! I flicked the lights on and told her to take a breath. 'What is wrong?' I asked.

"She looked at me with tears in her eyes and took a moment, trying to come up with the words to say. 'Mom, I think I have cancer or another disease or I think I am dying! Someone needs to help me!'

"'WHAT?! Tell me why you think this,' I said to her.

"She told me that she checked out her lady parts and was shocked by the sight of her vagina. 'It is just terrible down there! It has a lump inside it, and something doesn't seem right, so I googled some shit, and well, I think I am dying!'"

Now, my response was utter laughter at first. Then embarrassment. Then I realized I'm Lori freakin' Mork. I have seen many vaginas in my lifetime, and I don't need to be uncomfortable talking about the fact that some of us, myself included, might actually think their vagina isn't some glorious hole of greatness! Just sayin'! Show of hands, where are my not-so-confident ladies at? Who really believes their vagina is some temple to be shown off to the masses and studied for possible awards? I actually know women who do just that, and their confidence is off-the-charts magnetizing.

No woman has died from hating the appearance of her vagina!

Yep, go ahead, screenshot this, take a picture, and share this truth on your socials. You know it's true.

No woman has fallen ill or dropped dead because her cooch wasn't pretty. (And who made *these* standards anyway? Who decided which vag wins the trophy?! Society and Pornhub . . . that's who!)

Melissa continued. "I asked her to show it to me. She gasped, so I said, 'Um, I gave birth to you OUT OF MY VAGINA. I am certain it's okay for me to see yours.' She was reluctant and embarrassed; I mean the last thing she wanted to be talking to her mom about was"—Melissa whispered this part—"her *vagina.*"

Melissa kept going: "When she finally let me look, I realized everything was fine. She had a 'normal' vagina. So I asked her, 'Um, why do you think something is wrong with it? It's a vagina!'"

Okay, friends, let's get real and reflect a bit more about the good old honeypot! They aren't that stunning when you think about it. I mean, they serve a purpose in keeping the population of the earth going. Sure, sure, we use them for other things, wink, wink. #holla But the existence of them was literally to have a hole to get the sperm in, get pregnant, grow a baby, and have an exit plan for said baby when the nine months of free rental space was up. I don't think it was something that was thought about in terms of aesthetics. *Is this pretty enough? Should it have some sparkles and maybe a rose gold backdrop?* I have seen a ton of vaginas and no two look the same. Some are big, some are small, some are light, some darker, most are not like the ones you see in porn. Although they can be purchased for a price! I tell it like it is!

Melissa explained all of this to her daughter. Heidi looked relieved but also disgusted about having an "ugly vagina."

Shouldn't we as women have learned in school that "ugly" vaginas are the norm, and they still function perfectly well for what they're meant to do? Wouldn't it have been so much better if we had all been told when we were in preschool, "This is your va-jay-jay . . . and it looks *meh,* not bad"? It's not supposed to be like an oceanfront condo with a view—it's for a purpose. There are lumps, bumps, curves, edges, and it ain't all pretty. Likewise, there needs to be an additional lesson: "And this is your clitoris. It's REALLY important, and it also comes in many varieties!" It doesn't look like it belongs there, but it does and it's yours. Enjoy the heck out of it! So own it, and don't fret 'cause any man (or woman) lucky enough to look at it ain't thinking it's ugly. It's your vagina, and it's the key to greatness!

Rescue your own damn self by realizing that vaginas rule the world regardless of their appearances, and live sassily ever after!

Namaslay, Bitches!

Yes, that's right, let's slay and get into our asanas and make sure our inner world matches our outer world.

In an ideal world, I'd be contorting into all sorts of yoga poses and be Zen AF! Seriously!

But here is my great yoga debacle: I suck at it!

You read that right. I am a certified yoga instructor. I can lead a class, no problem. I can get everyone feeling calm and grounded. But when it comes to sitting still myself, I can't stay in one place. My mind has a hard time shutting the fuck up, and when it decides to join forces with my body, it's like it's 3 a.m. at a rave. I am *that* girl in yoga class! You know, the one in the back of the class, eyes wide open during savasana (which is corpse pose—supposed to be still body and still mind). I run through my grocery list: milk, check; cheese, check; eggs, check. I continue to glance around the room, enviously eyeing up all of the calm souls and wondering if they are snoring or actually doing this whole thing right.

I am also not flexible thanks to decades of weight training (which makes muscles tight and short). So when I first attended classes, I just didn't get what all the hype was about. Did people actually enjoy yoga, or did they just go there to hit up the hot male instructors or make it a singles' party? Or did they want to be part of the lululemon club? You know, head-to-toe lululemon gear, with matching mat and towel, complete with the brightest colored mani/pedi to coordinate. Is yoga really that essential in being happy or having this fab life?! Damn straight. And I will tell you why.

Yoga isn't about touching your toes; it's the journey to get there! It's true. I learned this while undergoing yoga teacher training. I realized I was doing it wrong all along. I also learned that not all yoga is the same. Not all yoga is for everyone, and we have to try different varieties of yoga to find what works for us.

I was always more of a badass yogi. Like I want to walk into that class and make it my bitch! I wanna sweat and work hard a little, but not too hard. I wanna flow, but not too much power (that's what the weight room is for). I want to stretch a little, and I want to feel like a warrior goddess. Then I wanna lay in savasana and think of how badass I am. And then I want out of there! I also came to terms with the fact I'm also a yin yoga kinda gal 'cause I like pain and anguish. I like to sob my eyes out in class! And yin yoga takes you deep into the feels while stretching your muscles and strengthening your patience.

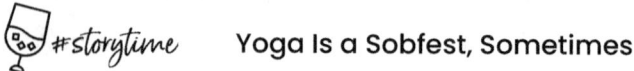 #storytime　**Yoga Is a Sobfest, Sometimes**

I was once in a yin yoga class, which in other words means hold the pose for like a million minutes, and just when you are ready to lose it, it's time to find another pose and hold it for what seems like eternity. More like four minutes, but it feels like days! A pigeon pose is a super intense hip opener, and we are all tight in our hips. But when I learned the hips were also our emotional center, I didn't believe it. "You mean to say we hold trauma and emotions in our hips?!" I call #bullshit. Or how about #trauma? Nope. Me? Traumatized? Not me. #denial #idonthaveanytrauma

I took my yin yoga teacher training and that was the day I finally realized I was holding a shit ton of emotion and trauma and it was about to come crashing down like Niagara Falls. As I moved into pigeon pose and held it (actually called "sleeping swan" in yin terms, but I don't know who could ever be sleeping. It's painful, and it's an emotional experience like no other, when you let it be!), I could feel the dam about to burst. Hello, sobbing mess Lori. Around minute two, I really started to release. My mind felt clearer, until it wasn't. I had this mega hot flush come over my body, tingly all over, then WHAM! Waterworks! I am not talking a little teary. I am talking sobbing, snotty, can't stop, ugly crying, complete mess. For about ten minutes, this waterfall of tears continued. Heck, everyone else moved on to the next leg, and I was still crying. I released a ton of shit, and on that very day, I was convinced why we *need* yoga to be rescued and live our life as a mega fairy tale!

I was no longer a naysayer! I was no longer a "it has to be a

Flow class" groupie or just a weight room junkie. I realized that we all need yoga. But are we all ready to let yoga be WITHIN us? You see, when you find the right kind of yoga, it goes deep inside you. It's not just about getting more flexible. It's not just about being still. It's about this journey you take yourself on. A quest for purpose, passion, inner peace, deep certainty. **A full body fuck-yes-I-love-myself-no-matter-what type of self-love.** And there is a type of yoga for everyone. Yin is amazing for emotional trauma and of course flexibility. Hatha is a gentle form that is super easy for anyone to do and just feels good. Flow or power is for you "can't sit still" types to get tricked into doing yoga while convincing yourself you're doing more than yoga. Then you can get even crazier and add things like goats or puppies to the mix, or beer yoga (heck, we are grasping here to sell yoga to the masses). I even took a happiness yoga class where we burst out laughing as loud and hard as we could for an hour. But my point is: try it, try it again, suck at it, get a little better at it, then hate it, then get better at it, then find the classes you like, then find the instructors you like, then find your groove in it, then let it work its magic.

You don't need to be fluent in Sanskrit or understand every single aspect of it to start. You just need to come to your mat with an open mind and no worries of any judgers (no one else cares what you are doing). Do the poses that feel good, or just lay in savasana and breathe.

Rescue your own damn self with badass yoga (or just regular yoga—I am trying to liven this party up a little with some badassery), breathe a frick ton, inhale gratitude, love, and hope, and exhale the bullshit, and live sassily ever after.

Newton Was Right, and Why Didn't I Pay More Attention in High School Science Class, Damn It?!

....

This chapter or life lesson is dedicated to all of the high school science teachers out there or—who am I kidding—any teacher who had to deal with the "Lori attitude" in my teen years!

Remember science class in high school? That's when I could be found protesting against dissecting frogs and pig legs; I was taking a stance for the vegan movement. This from a girl who ate chicken and wore leather. Clearly, I didn't comprehend what my stance really was. But there I was, outside the principal's office, refusing to dissect anything, and protesting the inhumanity. Heck, I think I took offense to the "fruit fly experiment" as well. "Save the fruit flies!" Jesus, my teachers were saints!

Okay, focus Lori, back to physics, where I could also be found flirting with boys, socializing by making plans for my weekend, passing notes, and eye rolling any time an adult spoke.

The fact I could even remember the name "Isaac Newton" baffles me. But I was writing this life lesson and it popped into my mind so I figured I should bring out my inner Miss Smarty Pants.

Newton is all about actions and reactions. For every action, there is an equal and opposite reaction. Whew, my scholarly work here is done.

 #storytime

Newton's Law as Applied to Life: Use Your Words and Your Voice Wisely

Interactions happen every day. We don't live on this earth alone. We share space with others and have to breathe the same air as them. How we interact greatly impacts how others respond. How we treat others will impact how they treat us back. "Don't do something to others you wouldn't want done to yourself!" and "You can dish it out but can't take it!" are both good examples of this scenario. My nemesis of the world today is "social media interactions." Keyboard trolls, hiding behind their screens, typing anything they want. Random strangers we consider "friends," allowed to interact with us daily, unfiltered! Most actions on social media aren't precisely planned out, thought out, or played out. You see a post, you react and comment, then the back-and-forth interaction, usually negative, is exchanged. It's maddening and tiring! I once posted a pic of one of my beautiful clients who had lost over twenty-five pounds from working with me. I posted a side-by-side selfie of her face before and after. I was posting it to show how happy she looked afterward. It had nothing to do with her NOT being pretty before. An ex-client of mine went off on a rage about her not looking any different, that she was pretty before, that makeup and lighting can make a difference in cheekbones, etc. I stopped reading since it was complete bullshit and a waste of too many seconds of my life! As I went to react and respond, I remembered I was writing my book. Newton's Law. So, instead of this massive retaliation, I merely posted, "I think you missed the point!"

You see, interactions happen every day, but if we can stop, pause, and breathe, then think things through, maybe we can avoid some of the toxic ones.

I apply this principle to those social media interactions, as well as real-life ones. Texting is often taken the wrong way, and the "lol" you type or the heart emoji you insert after typing something that might be misread as offensive leaves that imprint on someone, causing their reaction. Communication is something many of us struggle with every day of our lives, like learning how to respond properly or learning how to keep our emotions in check. The one I need help with is to "Take a deep breath and don't send the eight-page email or angry text before you can think about it for a while first!" In my interactions, I learned I needed to not send emotionally overwhelmed Lori responses. I need to first step away from the iPhone, walk the dogs, breathe, maybe formulate some pros and cons notes, then respond later. Lori's other big rule here: NEVER EVER text or respond after you've gotten into the Pinot Grigio, a bottle or so in, when you have some witty comeback or some beef to lay out to your man. You will thank me later! #thathappenstomealot Most of the time after cooling off, or sobering up, I don't need to respond at all, or I'm much more calm if I do.

#storytime Newton's Law Applied to Life: Consequences of Actions

Beyond the words we speak, the physical actions we take have reactions and consequences.

Think about drinking alcohol and getting behind the wheel of a car as an example. You have a good time partying, have way too many bevvies, and decide you are "okay" to drive home. Right there, by choosing that decision, you have invited reaction or potential consequence into someone else's life! You are making that choice to put your own self at risk, but at the same time, you're impacting anyone who might be crossing paths on your route home.

We see these choices and decisions result in tragic consequences, time and time again, when the drunk driver, who took that action, inevitably hits an innocent person's vehicle (reaction to being intoxicated and drinking) and the other person is injured or killed.

Just as we need to sit back and think about the words we speak or the responses we might type in a text, we have to remember the physical actions we also take always have consequences.

In high school, someone very special to me lost his life in the most tragic way. Travis was an amazing guy, who was actually one of my first crushes in grade seven. He was my first real kiss, and I can still remember his braces! Ouch! We remained great friends as we went on to high school, and he was often there to wipe my tears as I cried over many random loser guys who broke my heart. He was there to make sure I made it into the cab at parties when I was drunk and falling over. He was there to check in with me in the hallway when I looked frazzled, and he always made me feel better with his funny ways. I was on a family vacation one year when I got news about him passing away (which to this day, I still get choked up about every time I think of it). On August 2, 1993, we lost this amazing soul. I had missed a great party at a nearby cabin in the woods that many of the grade twelve students attended. Travis was with another friend, and they decided to take a canoe out on the lake. Without life jackets. In the wee hours of the dark night. Now, for most of us, this wouldn't be something we need to really think about too much in terms of consequences. While not totally safe, it should be fine, right? Well, Travis didn't know how to swim. I remember conversations with him many times about his inability to tread water. The canoe hit a wave and flipped, tossing them both into the water. Now, even to someone who can swim, it would be a difficult task to tread water, in the dark, while waiting for someone to find them, when no one knew they were gone. The other friend could swim, but sadly he was not able to continue to hold Travis above water as well as himself. I wish I could say the consequence of this action is the loss of Travis alone. You see, the other teen boy had to take that reaction, witnessing the death of his friend right next to him, seeing Travis's baseball cap floating beside him, but being unable to save him, for life! The emotional and psychological consequence of this is haunting. *To my dear friend, Travis, rest in peace. I think of you often! xo*

Accidents happen for sure, but just imagine how terrible shit could be averted in life if we could just sit back and take that mama bear role more often. If we could be intentional and think long and hard about how our actions, words, and reactions could impact each other.

Like a helicopter parent at the playground telling her toddler to be careful or they might fall, it's foreshadowing to see that a certain action could end up resulting in something happening. To see the future, almost like an *X-Men* character.

If I do this *action*, there might be a *reaction*, and there is a potential for this *consequence* to happen.

Rescue your own damn self by remembering Newton's Law in everything you do, and live sassily ever after!

Cinderella

Of all the fairy tales, this is my favorite. It's also probably the one that will stand out the most to us ladies. You see, growing up, I often used this fairy tale as my "dream come true" goals. Meet a handsome man, fall in love, get married, and be so freakin' happy. Whenever life would throw curve balls at me—guy is terrible to me and breaks my heart—this type of narrative always played in my head: *Don't worry, Lori, your time for your prince will come one day!* Like was I really thinking some hot guy would show up at my doorstep on a horse and rescue me from hurt and pain, and we'd live our happy life together?! I truly blame this fairy tale alone for my warped images of what love was supposed to look like and my unrealistic expectations of how I would find that love. Like it's just gonna be *THAT EASY*!

Lori's *Fast and Furious* Fairy Tale Breakdown:

* **Cinderella** loses her mother at a young age, then her father remarries an evil woman with two poorly mannered brat daughters. The father dies tragically,

leaving Cindy with this nightmare of a household keeping her as a slave and hostage.

✳ At the castle's Big Ball, the handsome **Prince** will be selecting his new bachelorette with a rose ceremony. (I watch a LOT of reality TV!) Everyone is going, but the evil stepmom locks Cindy away and says she can't go after all, playing with her emotions and letting her think she was going in the first place! (Don't forget, the birds and mice helped Cindy make her dress. Yep, that can happen in real life!)

✳ Cindy cries in the backyard, inserting the magical appearance of her **Fairy Godmother** who sends her to the ball in a beautiful gown and glass slippers with a pumpkin turned into a carriage and mice into horses. There was also a rule that at the stroke of midnight all of Cindy's lavish shit would disappear and she'd look homeless again.

✳ She meets the prince, they dance, and just from that one dance, they fall in love. Cindy literally falls head over heels as the clock strikes midnight. She heads for the hills to get the heck outta dodge before the prince finds out she's a fake, and one of her glass slippers falls off.

* The prince is lost without her so he searches through all the land, and in desperation, he proclaims that he will marry whoever can fit that glass slipper, making her his princess.
* He visits every home, but Cindy is hidden away by her evil step mama. But the prince persists and finds her. She tries the shoe, and it's a perfect fit. He rescues her from a life of abuse and marries her. They live—you guessed it—happily ever after in his posh castle.

The Facade or Complete Insanity in a Nutshell:

* I am still waiting for the day when my dogs decide to sing with me and help me clean my house or make clothing. That would be amazing! How can we buy this image of birds opening curtains and mice sewing? We surely need more household pets pitching in!
* A Fairy Godmother! Really? I have been waiting for mine my whole life. Some old lady who just shows up on my back patio and turns my rags to riches. But please, no glass slippers, I want Manolo Blahniks! #sexandthecityfanforlife

- Finding true love and our soul mate after one dance? A real relationship of substance takes proper time and commitment to strengthen.
- Did no one recognize Cindy at the dance? Was that another spell? Like when no one knows Clark Kent is Superman, just 'cause he has glasses on? I'm not buying it!

Lori's Revamp of this Madness—*Cinderella*, Take 2

Hold up, Lori, I am not a total skeptic. I do know people who meet some random person and just have this gut feeling it's their "person." I want to still hold onto some little bit of romance and dream. But . . . let's take a Lori spin on this one, for fun!

Plot Twist #1—Cindy's dad passes away, and he made sure he had a will that said SHE got the castle and her stepfamily is out on their asses! Legit, a good reminder to us all to make sure we have our affairs in order in case something ever happens to us. I'm leaving everything I have to my dogs!

Plot Twist #2—The Fairy Godmother is really a badass girlfriend, who comes over and says, "Girl, we need to get your hot ass to that ball to meet the prince! I got you!" She brings her best slutty

Vegas dresses (you know, the ones that can only be worn in Vegas, illegal in all the other states) and dolls her up. She sends her to the ball without a curfew. "Stay out all night, girlfriend. Remember what happens in Vegas stays in Vegas, or in the castle in this case!"

Plot Twist #3—Cindy does fall in love with the prince, but instead of racing away at midnight, she tells him who she really is. Speaking her truth. Sharing her story. Boldly. Here is the life lesson of not putting on that fake front for people. Own who you are. Shout it from the rooftops, and if someone doesn't like you for the real you, fuck 'em! If that prince really did fall hard for her, he would have said, "I love you anyway. Now, let's get you out of that abusive household and put a ring on it!" In life, we see fake images all the time: filters on social media, then meeting the person face-to-face and thinking, *wow, you weren't selling how you really looked!* Dating profiles with your pic from fifteen years ago, or heck, maybe it's someone else's photo. Don't lie about who you are when you're trying to find that perfect partner. It would be complete bullshit if I said that I loved hiking to find some nature-loving guy who'd learn the truth once he got me halfway up the mountain and I collapsed and curled up in a ball on the ground screaming, "HELL NO—I was just trying to sound adventurous!" You be you, Cindy, and if that prince isn't still smitten with you, I say, "Next!"

Plot Twist #4—Who here can run in high heels? Especially ones made of glass? Legit, this was the one thing I needed to change for certain. Midnight is striking. Instead of running in those heels, perhaps the Fairy Godmother should have equipped her for that sprint with a sparkly pair of sneakers! Maybe she is running in heels, and when she loses a shoe and her carriage turns back into a pumpkin, she calls an Uber, and heads home to drink a bottle of wine with her pet mice! My favorite idea of her getaway is what I've had to do many times for my besties. I get the call from the date she's on: "This is a bust, come get me!" So, I head to rescue her, we have drinks and go dancing instead, without any princes in sight 'cause we are swearing off men!

Maybe Cindy didn't really need the prince after all. I mean, she has free labor from working mice, and a magical Fairy Godmother on speed dial on her iPhone.

Rescue your own damn self by believing in true love but remembering to speak your truth, wear the comfy runners, and realize that your dog or mice aren't gonna clean your house, and live sassily ever after!

They Are Tampons, Sista, Not Grenades!

 **#storytime** **The Great Tampon Adventure**

Picture it: Vancouver, Canada, 2020.

Entering the grocery store to purchase tampons. Yep, you guessed it, it was that time of the month, and I'd run out of my stash. So, I walked in, only needing one thing and one thing only. Plugs! Now, normally I would have purchased ten to twenty other products because, hello, I can't just be seen roaming the aisles with a big box of tampons under my arm. But not this day. Oh no, this was the day I said, "I refuse to do that. I refuse to be ashamed when good old 'Aunt Flow' comes to visit. She is here. She shall be witnessed. Shame has no room here. I only need one thing, and one thing I shall get!" I picked up that blue-and-orange box with "super" written in huge, bold writing and headed to the checkout counter. I made it my mission to make eye contact with every person who crossed my path on this journey to period freedom. To note: One woman looked clear into my eyes with an expression of "You go, girl!" Another woman looked at me with affirmation: "This woman is our fearless leader." They knew the embarrassment we've all felt during our menstrual cycle. I get sick to my stomach thinking about how all those years as a teen I had to pretend I didn't get a period. Like I have a vagina, folks, that bleeds. Do you not remember learning this in grade seven sex education class?

#storytime   The White Pants

Allow me to share with you the story of the white pants. I was in Mr. Long's grade eight music class, and I remember it like it was yesterday. My friend Jodi stood up to go use the restroom, only to hear a cascading wave of gasps from all thirty idiotic preteens in our class as she walked past them. You guessed it, she was wearing white pants and she had just gotten her period for the first time (insert scary horror music here). I was disgusted at the reaction of all the kids around me. I quickly took off my cardigan (yes, I wore a cardigan; don't judge me, it was the '80s!) and lent it to her. She wrapped it around her waist so she could avoid hiding in her locker. You know what pissed me off the most? They called her "white pants" and taunted her for months. Like it defined her middle school existence. Unpopular opinion: Kids can be harsh and cruel sometimes, and often this is a learned behavior (#parentingfail). The same applies for any social taboos and stigmas we hold onto so tightly, like our menstrual cycle. Ladies, repeat after me: We have vaginas. We bleed once a month (sometimes more, depending on our hormone health). We are fierce creators who give life to all the world's human population, so why have periods become such a disturbing issue for men or even us gals?

#storytime · The Great Tampon Adventure . . . The Saga Continues

Okay, back to my quest in the great tampon adventure. I headed to the cashier to pay for my box of tampons. I really felt like a lone wolf at that moment. Super tampons for a super woman! #freetheperiod The women were proud, shocked, and in disbelief. But the men who accidentally made eye contact were not sure what they got themselves into. One man ran headfirst into the stack of dinner rolls on the end of the aisle. WHAM! Another man quickly looked away, for fear of cracking a smirk or showing his disgust. *She is bleeding? Gross!* (Insert massive eye roll here, like c'mon people, are we ten years old?!)

It was time to end this journey. Of course, I would go to the checkout lane that had a male teenager working at the cash register. I'm a glutton for punishment! As he scanned the big "super" box, I assumed he was just wishing I would quickly add some gum, a few candy bars, anything other than these alien invaders.

Just as I was ready to wrap things up, he finally mustered the courage to ask me, "Would you like a bag for five cents?"

Time for me to flex my power once again. "No thanks, I got this!"

I continued my quest to the parking lot with my large box of tampons in full view for all. No bag, no embarrassment. Just the balls I grew from not giving a shit and going after the prize of my womanhood.

That was the day I took control of **owning the shit out of being a woman AND having a period.** I rocked the fact I bought tampons and wasn't afraid of what anyone thought.

Rescue your own damn self from the tampon-judgers, own those tampon purchases, and live sassily ever after! You are She-Ra, the Princess of Period Power! Own that unapologetically!

I'm Exhausted from Reaching for the Moon!

Les Brown once said, "Reach for the moon, even if you miss, you'll land among the stars."

This was my life motto and mantra for years.

I used this in my business in terms of telling people to set big goals.

I used this in my personal life to always make myself aim high, think huge, dream big!

I used this in everything I did.

Reach! Focus on the biggest thing you can, then manifest it to happen.

Problem was, I was exhausted from always reaching.

I was always "failing" because I was setting my sights so high that I could barely hang on or see them.

Anything smaller than the dreams or goals I had for myself was less than! Like I just was never "good enough."

I was in my local hair salon a few months back, and as I went to the washroom, I looked up on the wall and saw a plaque that read "Dream Big!"

I felt myself massively eye rolling. That was my aha moment.

Why can't we "Dream Simple" or "Dream with Realism" or "Take Baby Steps" instead of giant leaps?

Set smaller goals and attain those. Little ones or easier ones to find success in.

I think of a meme I saw online once of two ladders side by side. One had normal rungs, about ten inches or so apart. The other ladder had only two rungs, one at the bottom and one way up at the top, showing how impossible that one would be to climb. The regular smaller steps are what help us to finally get to the top. Small steps toward our goal taken with intention create a big impact. It compounds over time.

In our careers, we can set smaller, achievable business goals, then keep pushing ahead. I think of when I opened my fitness studio. It was 4,000 square feet with three separate studios and twenty-two staff offering forty-five classes a week. It was way too much, too soon. Had I started smaller, there would have been fewer costs in terms of rental space, fewer members would have been needed, and I wouldn't have crumbled and gone bankrupt!

In relationships, I think of my friend Kerry. She would always jump into new relationships with two feet and no net, scaring off the potential lover with her big plans. "WTF, I just met this girl and she's picking out her wedding dress and the location for our honeymoon!" Had she just focused on the fun dating part of getting to know the other person, she wouldn't be sending potential mates running for the hills as she talked about them watching their future grandkids play! Baby steps, gurl! Back up, sister!

When a child learns to walk, we don't put them on a tightrope without that safety net and tell them to time themselves to get across it. First, they learn to crawl, then we hold their hands as they take their first steps or use a baby walker. Ease in! Slow and steady progress so they don't fall off the high wire.

In fitness or body goals, this can also ring true. Setting massive goals like losing one hundred pounds is scary and often leads to losing hope and patience and quitting. But by setting smaller milestones, you hit them, crush them, and keep forging ahead to getting better and better. Success!

Rescue your own damn self by thinking of all the ways in life you can dream a little smaller, succeed a little more, and live sassily ever after!

Orgasm Often, Holla!

There is nothing more powerful than the female orgasm! Nothing more amazing than your body reaching that full climax, when every inch of you is quivering and you're unable to speak. Nothing better than feeling fierce, sexy, feminine, and wild. And oh, that release!

Is it hot in here?

Do I have your attention?

Show of hands, who enjoys the big O?

No, not Oprah, I'm talking about a good old orgasm.

This is my favorite chapter. Yep, I'm playing favorites.

Female sexuality and female pleasure are just not talked about often enough, except over ample amounts of Pinot Grigio (with ice) with my girlfriends. We go there; we talk about SEX! We talk about good sex, bad sex, sex that is funny, sex that is mind blowing, and masturbation when we take charge and get down to business ourselves. Hey, men are allowed to brag about getting off constantly, so I am all over dispelling this taboo or urban legend that says we ladies can't embrace our sexual energy and talk about cumming!

I really do believe that many of the wars, disagreements,

murders, accidents, meltdowns, and insanity would be rectified or avoided if we just had that release of a powerful orgasm before we acted.

Stress would be a hell of a lot lower for a lot of people if they just bought the newest hot ticket sex toy and had at it!

Stop counting sheep to get to sleep for your "tossing and turning" and instead grab the bullet or rabbit or dildo, or if you are lucky to have Brad Pitt (or your real partner) lying next to you, mount them, and explode into sweet dreamland!

Forget vitamin C, orgasm and stay healthy! Yes, it's hella good for your immune system, because, hello, feel-good endorphins, balanced hormones, physical touch, and connection!

Have you ever met someone in a bad mood after they've had an orgasm? Legit! This is the time to ask your partner for that lavish vacation or new puppy 'cause they are freakin' happy! Endorphins are raging! "Sure, Lori, you can get that new sports car you have always wanted!"

Quit dieting and just have more sex. That is the best fitness advice I can ever give you—and I am a trained professional. An orgasm alone can burn like one hundred calories, throw in some rolling around, doggy style, etc., . . . sorry . . . what was I sayin'? Right, like 500 calories for a good sex session! Who needs a treadmill or the weight room? Bench me, baby, and have that tight, lean body! All thanks to achieving the big O!

#truthbomb: Some women have never experienced a true orgasm. Shut your mouth, Lori! This is worse than world hunger! I am taking on this new philanthropy in helping women everywhere enjoy more orgasms. Here is your gentle reminder to orgasm more. "Lori told me you have to make me cum 'cause I need to burn some calories!" I give the best homework for your partners! Just as you think it's enough, times that by two! I don't think anyone ever died from cumming too much! Do the research and get back to me!

My favorite thing about the big O is that you don't need anyone else for it! Sure, I will have an orgasm with someone else any day over the solo event, but it's not necessary. In fact, many of my friends prefer the art of masturbation over sex with someone else because then you're in control of your own orgasms! #alsolessdrama

 *#storytime*   **I Need to Climax, Damn It**

Years back, my client Tina was fresh out of a thirty-year marriage. She was on the prowl again. Hitting the dating pool with her vagina blazing. She met Greg, who was fifteen years younger than her and an Italian stallion. I remember during one of our sessions, she confided in me, "Lori, I am terrified to sleep with him. I slept with the same man for thirty years, and not once did I orgasm." It was something she struggled with for three decades. You see, in her family, masturbation was frowned upon in the eyes of the church (don't take me to that church, my friends!), so she went through most of her life not knowing that release or big O.

Well, I wish I had a happy ending to this one, but Tina orgasmed, exploded, and died! I'm kidding! Seriously, Tina slept with Greg, and he was not only good, he was great. Totally in tune with her needs. He knew what the clitoris was and where to find it! (That's for a whole other chapter: *The Quest to Find the Clitoris. A Journey of a Thousand Men*!) Greg was also a giver, and he gave and gave and gave. But Tina also stopped the madness of not expressing what made her feel good: "There, right there, to the left, to the left more, slower, lighter . . ." And release!

Expressing what you want, need, like, and LOVE is beyond important with a partner. I coached Tina until she was 71 years old, and I am happy to report that until the day she died, she made sure to orgasm often! Because once you have the big O, there is no going back to playing small! There is no leaving the game! You are in it to win it! There are many mediocre things in life. Sex shouldn't be one of them. Sorry, I need to go have a cold shower now.

Life's too short to keep having middle-of-the-road, lackluster, non-orgasmic sex. Rescue your own damn self by having tons of life-changing orgasms, and live sassily ever after!

Notting Hill

Oh, Julia Roberts, what would you do without the old romantic comedy genre? She's a rock star when it comes to helping us believe some of this nonsense, and we love her for it! Some of the best on-screen romances had her infectious cackle of a laugh and her beaming smile in them.

Notting Hill plot:
- Poor, barely making ends meet, bookstore owner (Hugh Grant) falls for super popular, rich Hollywood actress (Julia Roberts).
- They fall for one another instantly and sleep together (of course!).
- Insert heartbreak. Not just once, but multiple times she breaks his heart. Stomps on his heart, actually. Poor dude.
- In the final scene (just like in every romantic comedy, the boy and girl live happily ever after), she shows up again at his bookstore, claiming she's "just a girl standing in front of a boy, asking him to love her." Insert Lori and her waterworks! #missemotional

- He does choose to love her, they kiss, roll credits, happily ever after!

Yeah, I don't buy this one. I need a rewrite for sure. Or possibly a few different real-life scenarios I can see playing out instead of just being loved again.

You see, we need to rescue ourselves by realizing that our actions have reactions and implications that end up resulting in things not working out how we need or want them to.

We hurt others, usually not with intent, but we do. In this movie, Julia Roberts's character was the meanie! It wasn't the typical boy breaks girl's heart. The girl is a jerk to the boy many times, then assumes crying or pleading in front of him will make it all better. Don't be THAT girl. Treat every human with kindness and respect, heck, even the ones with annoying roommates, too many cats, and small penises. #whenyaknowyaknow Even if you are the one who messes up, own that shit, don't be a mean girl!

We have emotions. **We sometimes make mistakes in love. We often do things we look back on later and think, *oh fuck*! But we need to own that shit!** We need to take ownership of the hurt or upset we cause others. WE can be the villain sometimes too. "Who, me?" Yes, Lori, you! We sometimes shit the bed in terms of making someone feel less than. It happens.

But it's never too late to mend the broken hearts we have

trampled on. By making apologies. Owning it. Releasing it. Showing that person you fucked up big time and will do all you can to win them back. Or to make amends.

My rewrite goes something like this, and it does involve some heartbreak and life lessons:

Plot Twist #1—Girl standing in front of a boy asking him to love her. And he says, "Sorry, babe, it's too late." Maybe that ship has sailed, too much water under the bridge, the heart is too broken and beyond repair. Maybe the moral of this rewrite is that when we hurt someone, we might not get a second chance. Maybe the life lesson is that the boy says, "No, thanks," and the girl is now brokenhearted herself and has to pull up her big girl panties and own it. She needs to take this little chapter with her to her next relationship to ensure she isn't being some diva or idiot next time. Live and learn from one lost love, and don't make the same mistake twice. Our prior relationships shape us when moving ahead into new ones.

Plot Twist #2—Girl asks for that love and forgiveness, and he says, "Maybe." They need therapy and time to heal, ya know, to find their way back to one another. #therapyislife They need to repair the broken hearts. Take the time to fall back in love and make amends. Time to realize this amazing love IS worth fighting for.

Time to realize that most relationships require give and take, have ups and downs, and expensive therapist bills. Most relationships take work to keep the love strong. Needing to BE loved means working on yourself and working WITH the other person to ensure you are always moving ahead together. It's a team sport. Love takes constant effort and evolution. We screw up, then we can find forgiveness in mending wounds and working shit out.

Rescue your own damn self by learning to look within and reflect on your own actions, so you can grow, heal, own that shit, and live sassily ever after!

In a World Full of Cheerios, Be a Sassy Fruit Loop!

As I write this chapter, I can't help but recall Vancouver Pride Week that just took place not long ago, celebrating the LGBTQIA2+ community. I honestly feel like it's just one big fairy tale festival of goodness, love, energy, and acceptance—all in one amazing week.

The reason I love Pride Week is because you don't have to be in the community to partake, celebrate, bust out the rainbow speedo and boas, and strut your princess-diva-goddess-self alongside all the other badasses celebrating diversity. You simply come together in love, unity, and kindness to celebrate and have a kick-ass time!

I was introduced to the LGBTQIA2+ community at a very young age. One of my favorite older female relatives was happily in love with a woman, and they lived together. I remember knowing this before any of the adults around even told me. I think I was the one to break the news to everyone: "You know they aren't 'roommates,' right?!" I thank the Lord I was able to witness that being different is something that is okay, that we all don't have the same love, nor do we all need to "beat to the same drum." Many of my friends growing up were not as lucky. Their conservative families frowned on diversity. It was their way or no way. It was often talked about in negative tones among some of my friends' families. I would witness this and think, *Wow, aren't you gonna be in for a shock when you realize the world isn't filled with everyone being the same, loving the same, or doing the same as you!* I remember thinking *what the fuck* when people considered something wrong or taboo just because it wasn't something they'd do. #closedmindedmuch

I remember meeting people in high school knowing that they were struggling with their sexuality, and I was often the one they would confide in. I gave off the vibe of *no judgments* even back at that age. I allowed anyone coming into my circle to know it was a safe space with me. I learned people have different sexual orientations, and also that some of us didn't have a freakin' clue where we wanted to be or which box we fit into.

 #storytime   **Drag Queens, I Love You**

When I just graduated from college, I lived in a small Northern Ontario city with a lot of straight and narrow, close-minded, redneck assholes. #truestory One of my first real "boyfriends" was a guy named Stephan. He was this blond hunk of a man who would meet me at the gym for workouts and was just so in tune with everything I needed. Cooking me dinner was just the best! We hit it off right away and were inseparable. I honestly thought I would marry this man. More on how this plot twist took a rapid turn shortly!

For our first real date beyond the gym sessions, he picked me up and said with complete hesitation, "I have something we need to do to support one of my best friends, and I'm hoping you will be okay coming along with me for it for our date."

I grinned. I've always been known as the girl who is "up for anything!"

He didn't tell me what we were doing as we headed to one of the dark, dreary local hole-in-the-wall basement pubs. As we entered, I could see this color explosion of greatness. I could see smiles, bright eyes, happiness, glowing personalities, and I immediately felt I had been welcomed into some kingdom with MY people. The music was blaring my all-time favorite '90's dance party hits, there were sparkles and lights and glitter, and it was just pure raw, powerful, fun energy. I was at my first drag queen show. As one of the most beautiful queens approached our table, I saw her embrace Stephan. She then turned to me and gave me one of the biggest and longest hugs I have ever received.

"You must be Lori! I have heard so much about you. I'm Stephan's bestie, Richard, and, babe, I freakin' LOVE your black skirt! HOT! I need to know where you got it!"

I was in love with her genuine openness and with the aura of the room. Lock the door and throw away the key, I didn't want to leave. I wished life could be like this outside the four walls of this dirty pub! Stephan watched my face as I took in all the amazing performances. He could see I was hooked!

We partied the night away with all the queens, and to this day, I consider that to be one of the best nights of my life! As we drove back home, Stephan turned to me and said, "I have never met someone like you. You just don't see black and white, you see rainbows! In everyone and in everything. You make people feel like they are seen, and you make them feel like they are the most important people on the planet in a world trying to make them feel different or like they're nobody, and that is magical!"

Richard and I ended up being best friends for two years after that first meet-up. Even when Stephan and I parted ways, Richard and I became inseparable. He was in the nursing program, and he even pierced my navel (without freezing it properly for me! Ouch on that front!). He raided my closet (and now I'm wondering how my wardrobe fit his six-foot-tall muscular body?!), but hey, at the time, it was an honor. He's always had the same energy and sparkle about him!

What happened to Stephan? We had such a great relationship and friendship. Here's the juicy plot twist: Stephan is happily married with kids. He and his husband have two children. I remember him reaching out years after our split. And just like I was at that drag queen show that first night, I was immediately filled with acceptance and love. Although I did make him assure me that I wasn't the reason he swore off women! I've always wondered if some of my exes have exiled themselves and are living a life of celibacy after having to deal with me! #kiddingbutnotkidding

If you have never attended a drag queen show or a pride parade, I invite you to experience the magical adventure. I want you to go with an open mind and in an outfit you can only get away with wearing to these types of events (anything goes, just make sure the little bits are covered!).

This circle around me was and will always be a safe space. Everyone should feel free to be who they are. To feel free to be different. Be a freakin' fruit loop in a world telling you to be a Cheerio! No matter what you were taught about love, sexuality, and differences, I hope you live your life with an open heart and an acceptance that people aren't all the same or like you!

Rescue your own damn self by embracing your own inner colorful essence that makes you or those around you different, and live sassily ever after!

Patience Is a Virtue!

···

Hi, my name is Lori, and I have zero patience! Nada! Zilch!

Waiting for something—ugh, don't sign me up for that!

Enduring something with a long-time commitment and my ADHD kicks in and, "Oh look, a squirrel!"

Staying calm even though you know something is going to take longer than you thought makes me want to toss in the towel, wave the flag, and leave. I'm outta there!

Describe it how you want to, patience is really just being okay with shit taking time!

"Good things come to those who wait." Yeah, right!

I would like to brag about being cured of my impatience, but I am still one of the least patient people ever. I'm a work in progress and have tried to cultivate a little more patience, but it's hard. Trying to have more patience has made me a better person and a hoot to be around!

"Be patient!" We hear it all the time, but it's easier said than done, right? We want it, and we want it now! I saw a meme online that sums up my life. A woman is crying and the caption reads: "I've been dieting for four hours and don't have my dream body yet!"

#truthbomb: Epic shit doesn't happen overnight. That deep stuff takes time. It's a process, a journey, and sadly, it takes a whole shitload of patience and grace. It's not really the stuff of fairy tales: *Princess leaves on an epic quest to save the kingdom, but doesn't pack enough supplies, gets bored, and returns home empty handed in two days!* Or *The queen decides to start a new kingdom, but the building permits are taking too long so she quits and eats her body weight in nachos!*

 **#storytime**   **Kelly Finds Her Patience**

Relationships need to be on the patience train. My client Kelly would meet guys on Tinder (I swear I know all about these dating sites and have never been on them!). She would go out on lots of first dates, but none of them ever made it any further. She was a lifelong serial first-dater. I asked her why no second date? She was making judgments based on first impressions. When I told her she had to be more patient and give these handsome princes more of a chance, she agreed to become a third-date person. She would go on the first date and unless she was totally not feeling it, and unless they had sixteen things on her list of things she didn't like about them (yes, she had lists), she agreed to go on a second date. As she got to know them, if that list got down to ten things, she went on a third date. After that, for the most part, there were only a few things left on her list. By having patience and truly giving someone more of her time, she was able to see more clearly the bigger picture of what they were all about and whether there was potential for a future love affair.

The same applies for a new job or career. We start a new position, loathe it, hate it, cry, pour wine every night, and think of reasons to call in sick or scroll the ads to find anything different. But usually it's just the learning curve of something new. If we go by the six-month rule and stick it out for a bit, we usually find it's not that bad. By then, we're usually rolling along nicely, have made a friend we can joke with, and the job ends up being a long-term position. If we threw in the towel on day one or week one every time, we would be constantly on the hunt for a new job!

Business goals, fitness goals, and financial goals all require us to take that deep breath, take it day by day, and wait for the long-term results.

Time and patience. Repeat after me: P-A-T-I-E-N-C-E.

There will be times when you feel extremely frustrated. But if we can really focus on reframing our *I want it now* mentality, the good stuff does end up coming in the end.

Braving the troubles results in the princess slaying the dragon and saving the kingdom—eventually! As long as she doesn't get impatient and pack it in before the good shit happens!

Rescue your own damn self and know that a lot of life is about waiting and finding the patience to live sassily ever after!

Tame the Green-Eyed Monster!

....

"Don't let the green-eyed monster get you!"

Do you remember hearing this saying as a kid?

For years, I spent endless nights searching my closet for some evil, hairy, green monster that was hiding in there waiting until I was just about to drift off before it'd jump out and get me! Boy, our parents fucked us up with these sayings.

Jealousy and comparison (a.k.a. that green-eyed monster) often creeps into our daily life.

I'm exhausted from the years I spent thinking: *My ass isn't as tight as hers.* Or *I'm not as pretty as my friend.* Or *I don't have a nice house like my neighbor.* Or *I wish I had a great career and fun travel like her.*

The truth is, it's draining. It takes so much time and energy away from our lives to always be striving to be someone or something we aren't.

Social media, society, and our own little insecurities constantly engage us in the losing game of "who is better, richer, happier, more successful than us?"

I have a client who is a drop-dead gorgeous super-model-looking hot tamale. Men just fall over in front of her at her feet and cry "no mercy." Well, okay, maybe I tend to over exaggerate. But I used to spend my time with her picking myself apart, not seeing any flaws in her, but reflecting and magnifying all my imperfections. Through the years of coaching her, I realized that even she gets jealous of other women. It was hard for me to believe since all I saw was her beauty and perfect body. What I didn't see was her insecurity, her own self-confidence struggles, and her day-to-day comparisons of others who might have nicer clothes, more money, etc. It really is a never-ending hamster wheel for all of us. The comparison game will always leave you feeling defeated, so put down the Monopoly money and use your "get out of jail free" card and skip playing it!

I stopped allowing that green-eyed monster to take over my mindset by turning any comparison into a positive. I started to compliment others on the things that once had me attacking myself, and it made me feel so much better. I replaced the competition I was having with everyone around me with supportive feedback about all the great shit they had that I noticed. And I compliment myself too.

Now, any time I find myself comparing or envying, I compliment that person, then I remind myself of two great qualities I have. For example, my bestie Patti has amazing shoulders (she actually hates this about herself, but that's another story!). When I find myself eyeing up her perfect delts, I compliment her. I tell her how perfect her boobs look; she hates when people mention her shoulders. It's an issue for her! Then I remind myself of two things I love about myself: great ass and sexy eyes! Win-win for us both! She feels good, and I do too. I know that we aren't in some competition, so I can point out the things that I love about her, then I finish off with making myself see that we all have great qualities and features.

Rescue your own damn self by making friends with the green-eyed monster and ridding yourself of the spiral of endless comparisons, and live sassily ever after!

The Little Mermaid

I wish I were a mermaid! I've always loved the water, and having the ability to breathe and talk and live under the sea seems incredibly magical. *Who needs legs when you've got fins and can live in the ocean!*

Lori's *Fast and Furious* Fairy Tale Breakdown:

※ **Ariel**, who is a mermaid, is obsessed with leaving the ocean kingdom to head to dry land and become human—with legs!

※ Ariel finds **Prince Eric** washed away in the water after being thrown off his boat during a storm. She sings to him, and this magically saves him. Ariel leaves before he opens his eyes to see her for fear he would see she was just a mermaid, but he remembers the beautiful sound of her voice.

※ **Nasty Witch Ursula** (I told ya there is always a nasty queen or a witch in these fables) uses magic to give Ariel legs, and she promises that if Ariel could make

Eric fall in love with her (Ursula), Ariel's legs would become permanent. But the catch (there's always a catch with someone so evil) is that Ursula will take her voice (yes, that beautiful singing voice that Ariel needs to remind the prince of her identity). Legs in exchange for being unable to sing or even speak— that's a tough one!

* Devious Ursula turns herself into a beautiful maiden, and with Ariel's voice, she makes Eric fall in love with her, and they are to wed! Sneaky bitch! If you ever have friends who have #nomoralcompass, drop 'em like it's hot, for real!

* Ariel crashes that party and destroys the necklace that allows Ursula to have her voice. Eric realizes it's Ariel who he is in love with. But Ursula causes a bunch of storms and chaos. Thankfully, Ariel's father, **King Triton**, shows up with his posse and they kill the evil witch.

* King Triton grants Ariel her wish of legs, she marries Eric, and they live happily ever after!

The Facade or Complete Insanity in a Nutshell:

* Well, I'm just gonna say it and spoil the dream or

belief for you all. Mermaids aren't real! I really wish they were, but they aren't!

* Eric needs to raise his standards if he falls in love with a woman just 'cause she's a good singer! I mean, he hasn't even talked to her or seen her face. Legit, she serenades him while he's half dead, and that's all he needs to fall head over heels.

* Why didn't Ariel just ask her dad to switch her mermaid tail for some legs? I mean her dear old dad gives them to her in the end anyway, so think of the time and heartbreak that would have been saved by her just asking for what she wanted in the first place instead of beating around the bush or making shady deals that sound too good to be true.

* Yes, Ursula took Ariel's voice so she couldn't speak, but she could still communicate. Did she forget how to write? Like, gurl, write the prince a note: *Hey, handsome, I was the hot girl singing, but some mean lady cast a spell, so I can't speak. But I'm the one!*

* So, you're telling me this mermaid, with the beautiful blue ocean at her fingertips, wants to become human where she'd have to get a job and parent some little rug rats with some guy she actually hasn't spoken to. She knows nothing about him. He might not have a

brain, be a loser, or worse, is a serial killer. Stranger danger! She didn't even meet him. She rescued him by singing to him, then ran away for fear of showing him her true self. Sounds like a relationship with *lifelong love* written all over it! Or a *Dateline* episode about a romance gone wrong!

Lori's Revamp of this Madness—
The Little Mermaid, Take 2

Plot Twist #1—Ariel saves Prince Eric and instead of running away (no pun intended, get it, she can't run 'cause she's a mermaid, no legs!), she waits for him to wake up, they have a convo, she thinks, *Meh! Maybe being a mermaid ain't so bad.* I mean, men are complicated creatures, and in the ocean she has a nice friend who's a singing lobster. A much simpler life!

Plot Twist #2—Ariel actually stays and tells him who she is. They fall in love anyway, because he is accepting of her as a mermaid. He puts in a huge infinity saltwater pool in the backyard of the castle, and they merge both of their lives together as one! She doesn't need to change herself just for a man and lives happily ever after just being herself!

Plot Twist #3—Any *American Idol* fans out there? Ariel is singing to Eric, she saves him, and a top record producer hears her amazing voice, signs her to a two-record multimillion-dollar contract, and she moves to Vegas for a residency at Caesars Palace (the spa there could double as mermaid central!). She doesn't need some prince she's never spoken to.

Rescue your own damn self by owning what you got, working what your strengths are, and if all else fails, let's make the ocean our own and become a damn mermaid, and live sassily ever after! (Or just buy a slutty Mermaid costume for Halloween and pretend for the day!)

The Bikini Is Not the Enemy!

I'm just gonna drop a real quick #truthbomb right here before I start my storytelling. Repeat after me: **A swimsuit is not the enemy, it's *my* perception of my body *in it*!**

Raise your hands if you've ever put on a bikini and said "Bleh!" Or how about this . . . it's finally warm enough to wear one and you're excited to jump into that bad boy, but not even two seconds have passed before you look at yourself in the mirror and you LOATHE IT?!

Here's the thing . . . bikinis are beautiful! Swimsuits are sexy! If I could live in one all year round, I would. Heck, after roaming around in my birthday suit, a bikini is like being fully clothed to me! There are so many different styles, textures, and materials, and wearing one is an expression of feeling sexy, beautiful, goddess-like, and owning your body in all its glory—tiger stripes, curves, scars, and more!

The sad part is that society's and media's shitty ideals showcase the impossible standards we are still living with and allow into our minds. They tell us that we aren't beautiful in that bikini. (Don't get me started again on this one! UGH!) These standards shouldn't dictate our self-worth in that bikini!

 **#storytime**

Boating and the Self-Esteem-Killing-Machine

My client Sara checked in with me one Friday in July to tell me the story of dreading the bikini. You see, she and her hubby own a boat, and it was prime boating season. They were about to go out with a bunch of amazing friends, and she knew it would inevitably be a fun time! But for hours before the boat launch party, she sobbed. She was tempted to fake being sick to get out of the trip even though she knew that meant missing out on a really good par-tay! Truth is, she was afraid of being seen in a bikini. She looked for wraps and cover-ups, anything to try to make her feel better in it. But no luck. The stress and anguish that this little piece of clothing had over her existence was frightening. The bikini had become her *fun killer*! How did this thriller end? She realized that the boat would have all of her friends on it. Friends who loved her and saw her as kick-ass and beautiful no matter what. Heck, they were all gonna be drunk within the first hour anyway, so why did she even care?! So, she wore it and owned it and felt amazing! Her body didn't change, but her mindset did!

Moral of the story: Don't let any piece of clothing or anyone steal your joy!

 **#storytime**   **Water Babies Suck Ass**

To all my mamas reading this, you are not alone. You are beautiful. You are badasses! Heck, y'all grew, nourished, birthed, and sustained a whole human being (or more). So, why are we so ashamed of our bodies and their powerful magic during and after pregnancy?

Who has been with me on this? It's a few months post-delivery, and you signed your little cutie up for a nice little fun swim lesson called "Water Babies" at the local community pool. And you are excited, until . . . (insert the scary music from *Jaws*) you realize that *someone* has to actually be IN THE POOL with your baby. And lucky you, mama, with those extra twenty-five plus pounds of baby weight you still have yet to lose, and hips and a waistline that haven't found their shape again, it's gonna be YOU! Your self-esteem got tossed out with the placenta, so this ain't gonna end well! I sobbed hysterically for weeks leading up to that first class. I mean, was it postpartum depression or the fact that sleep was not happening? Or was it my lack of understanding that it really didn't matter what I looked like while I took my amazing baby to her first experience in a pool with other babies? But it ate at me. *I HATE THAT SWIMSUIT!* Then it dawned on me. The swimsuit never did anything to hurt me. *Why was I so negative about it?* When I released my thoughts and feelings around the swimsuit, I was finally able to just get on with it and relish the whole experience for what it was: splashing about in the water like a feisty mermaid with this amazing being I gave birth to. How lucky was I to watch her splash around in the pool for the first time? In that moment I stopped freakin' worrying about my body and blaming it for its lack of "perfection" in that innocent swimsuit. My baby surely didn't think twice about Mama's butt size!

It runs so much deeper than that skimpy piece of fabric. It's the skin you're in, sista! So start flipping the script of how you feel when you are in it. How would it feel if we worried less about our swimsuits and focused more on why we desired to wear them? What if we committed to never speaking an ill word about our bodies, no matter what the size or shape? What if we started to make ourselves put on the swimsuit with more kindness and respect for our bodies? Wouldn't that be fuckin' freeing?

Rescue your own damn self from being the bikini-body-judger, strap on that swimsuit and own it, and live sassily ever after!

Whoever Invented the "Trust Fall" Doesn't Understand the Concept of Trust!

....

Picture it: Grade four, and your teacher lines you up in a row next to half of your classmates, with the other half lined up directly behind you.

"I want you to fall back, and trust that the person behind you will catch you," says Mr. Parker. Yep, always a male teacher telling me to just trust some snot-nosed prepubescent boy who isn't paying attention to anything happening and is looking out the window daydreaming.

Seriously, you want me to trust some guy I barely speak to, who owes me nothing, actually probably doesn't even like me ('cause boys at that age don't like girls yet!), who is gonna think it's funny to show off to his friends and let my ass fall flat to the ground?! You are asking me to just trust that someone who I don't have any trust built up with will catch me just because you said so? Hard no! I never did it. Not once. I would take detention before I would give that power and control away to some "random."

Now, put my bestie, Patti, behind me, my soul sister, who I know would commit a felony to rescue or help me, and yep, I would fall back time and time again.

So, I am supposed to feel secure and confident that the person standing behind me isn't going to abuse that power?

I get it; trust should be just something you give to someone with the thought they'll behave the way intended. But man, oh man, life has taught me more than to trust that Mr. Parker telling some punk kid what to do won't result in my ass not hitting the floor. That shit has to be earned!

Trust is an emotion that takes time to build up! But that will vary from person to person and from situation to situation.

Trust can be earned, but it can also be broken and taken away with actions.

As I got older, I began to appreciate the *concept* of the "trust fall." Mr. Parker had great intentions, for sure. It was a team-building exercise. The problem was we were a bunch of kids who didn't really get the concept of trust yet. Plus, the exercise is a pretty stupid one, IMO!

I remember the "trust fall" being pushed on me again at an employee team-building event. I was a bartender at a nightclub in town. We had a big team meeting, and once again, we had to line up so the other half of the staff behind us would catch us.

I didn't do it. Ya know why? My "partner" happened to be an ex, who not only was a complete nightmare of a person, but he had broken my trust time and time again.

"I want a new partner!" I demanded. The bar manager looked

at me and said, "Lori, listen, you need to let him regain your trust. Do it!"

Nope, not happening. I still didn't understand who kept screwing up this concept of what trust was, how to earn it, how to keep it, and when to work on it.

 #storytime   **The Day I Finally Learned TRUST**

Trust didn't come easy to me. My therapist will tell you this is from my childhood and emotional baggage from the past. I'm sure that will be unpacked in my next book! Or in the mortgage payments I pay her for therapy!

I was actually unable to truly trust anyone until I became a mother. Trust was found in my gut (for some, this might be your head, or your heart—we carry these emotions differently, and mine is always my gut!).

I think it's when reality sinks in and tells you your actions will impact this little being. It's when you look at that tiny baby of yours and realize this brand new being has never had their trust broken. They trust you with their life, literally! You are keeping them alive. You haven't earned any trust! They just assume you have the best intention and interest in their well-being.

Was I wrong? Not me, I am never wrong. Was it that we are all born with trust, but the experiences, traumas, and life situations can break that trust or take it away?

Was it that we are all born with unlimited amounts of trust to just "fall back" into random strangers' arms and believe they will catch us, but year by year, fall by fall, the times we didn't get caught make us hesitant to keep "falling back," making it impossible for us to trust?

I flipped this narrative in terms of making others "earn my trust." I started by learning to give everyone a clean slate. New friends, new acquaintances got 100 percent trust from me, and they needed to show me they could keep it. I stopped believing past experiences with others would "happen again." I stopped punishing others for the broken trust from my past.

I learned to perform the "trust fall" every single day. I fall back into someone's arms, trusting they have the best intentions for me, trusting they won't let my ass hit the floor. I started to trust myself to know that if someone does break my trust, lets me fall, fail, or get hurt, that I have a massive chunky ass to land on to protect me when I do hit the floor. Have you seen it? It's gonna be an easily cushioned blow!

Take a leap off the trust mountain and fall back into the "trust fall" with optimism. Worst case scenario, if that trust does get broken, you will rescue your own damn self by knowing you can handle it, rise back up, and live sassily ever after!

Goddesses Don't Use Some Metal Object to Determine Their Self-Worth!

....

It's early morning and you bounce out of bed full of energy and a zest for life. You strip down and hop on the scale stashed in the corner. Just like that, as you glance down to see that number staring back at you, your mood can get flushed down the toilet. WHAM! It's higher than you thought, the day is ruined. It's not dropping like you wanted, the day is now set out to be an anger shitshow. The scale just told you that you're a terrible person!

You are a failure!

You are too heavy!

You are less than!

Why does one small object, made of metal, that doesn't tell us anything about how amazing we all are control our sense of being?

Your weight alone doesn't and has never given you the full picture in terms of health, wellness, and beauty! Yet it takes up space in our homes and minds everywhere!

I've been coaching for thirty years, and if I know one thing for certain, it's that **our relationship with the scale is a toxic one because the scale is a lying bastard!**

It's like an abusive relationship. You (the victim) feel pretty good about yourself, and the abuser (the scale) takes down any ounce of positivity to make you question your worthiness. The scale thrives on our weakness of already holding that number in high regard in terms of our body image or self-esteem. It knows we are struggling, and it kicks us when we are down, revealing its narcissistic qualities.

I could sit here and list all of the reasons why the scale sucks, but this isn't a "dissect the scale and toss it out" kinda book.

This is the life lesson of this scale bullshittery.

The quicker you smash, toss out, or just ignore the scale, the faster you will regain control of your self-worth, confidence, and own your body image!

The sooner you realize the scale sucks, the better life becomes.

 #storytime   **The Jello and the Rock**

I get it; we want to be fit! Most of us are all striving to be smaller, leaner, tighter, more defined. But the scale doesn't accurately represent this.

Picture a big blob of jello. It's light, airy, weighs very little, but it's jiggly and soft, and if we dig deeper, it has no real structure or substance to it!

Then picture a rock. Not Dwayne Johnson (although, yummy!). I mean like an actual rock from the garden. The rock is hard, perhaps smaller than that blob of jello, but it's compact, dense, and heavier! But the rock takes up much less space than the jello. The rock is strong. The rock has depth to it. The Rock is so sexy! (*Wait, I'm back to Dwayne Johnson again! Lori, focus!*)

Which would you rather be? The rock or the jello?

My greatest successes in my career as a fitness coach are when I help a woman break free from the madness of the weight scale. When she sends me her progress and measures it in how her clothes fit, how she's "feeling," and doesn't even care anymore about the number on the scale.

My greatest feeling of accomplishment is when a client says to me, "I don't know how much I weigh, and I don't care!"

#storytime Brenda's Breakthrough

My client Brenda was scale obsessed. She would sometimes weigh herself four to five times a day! She was so upset if she wasn't seeing progress with her weight. We had been coaching together for a month, and she was ready to quit. But she would also send me comments like: "I feel better" or "people are noticing I am looking smaller and leaner." She once sent me a check-in that said, "Wow, I fit into my clothes from ten years ago. I am my smallest!" Yet she still allowed the number on the scale to define if she was a success or failure. We finally broke free of that about two months in when she said to me, "Lori, I actually see what you mean; I don't think it's telling me an accurate number!"

We pretended it was broken. And went two more months coaching together. About four months into our training, she was still free of the scale, feeling amazing, and crushing personal bests for strength. She had also healed her relationship with food. I asked her if she wanted to weigh herself anymore. She replied, "That would be a waste of time and energy. I go by how I feel now, and I feel amazing. I thought about it a few times, and I wonder what weight I actually am when I feel this good. But then I realized it didn't matter. I knew that no matter what the number said, it would haunt me, so instead of thinking it was broken in the cupboard, I took it out and put it on the floor one last time. And instead of stepping on it, I released it. It's dead to me, so I threw it out. The ghost that was haunting me no longer has any hold over me. I know it has zero indication of how I am really doing, inside and out!"

To this day (five years later), she's never once thought of it since.

If you were in a relationship I thought was abusive to you, I would tell you. I would tell you to set yourself free and allow yourself to gain back control. Bye-bye, scale; hello loving yourself fully beyond numbers.

This doesn't mean we don't want to improve our bodies or

physiques. But do not allow that piece of crap to have the final say. Or any say, for that matter.

Rescue your own damn self from that nonsense spit out by some random number generator, and live sassily ever after!

Jerry Maguire

This bad boy of a romantic comedy has me hitting up a few life lessons . . . and sassy Lori plot twists.

But wait, you haven't seen this movie? Let me give you a quick rundown:

Jerry (Tom Cruise) hires cutie Dorothy (Renée Zellweger) to work for him when he quits a massive sports talent agent job and starts his own company. With zero clients, she follows him and his dream. They fall for one another, sleep together (of course), and he thinks he loves her. But we slowly see that Jerry is a self-centered prick focused on showing his clients "the money." So, they split because he thinks he made a mistake. He breaks her heart, but then thinks he can show back up on her doorstep and win her back with three little words. No, not "I love you," but "You complete me!" She tells him, "You had me at hello!" Love conquers all, and "completed," they live happily ever after!

Okay. Two things about this movie I need to rewrite or rip apart to provide a sassy life lesson for you.

First, "You complete me!" SAY WHAT? This notion that

anyone has *that* kinda power over us, that before we met them we were not ever whole and that we just aren't complete with anyone else is utter nonsense! Jerry stands in front of Dorothy after crushing her soul, leaving the single mom alone with her super cute little son with his super cute little glasses and wins her back by just saying hello?! REALLY?! Nope, that's way too easy!

Do we really think that little of ourselves that some self-obsessed guy with a flashy smile can get us that easily?! #timeforselfworthtalk

Plot Twist—He shows up and says the "completing me" bullshittery! And she makes him work for her forgiveness by him learning from his mistake (insert costly therapist appointments), and only then, after months, does she reconsider saving their relationship. But she doesn't complete him. The thought that any of us have that power over someone else is absurd. **We need to rescue our damn selves by knowing we have got this with or without anyone else.** No one gets me just at "hello." You've got to work for this goddess! Earn it! We can be extensions of one another, but this notion that anyone makes us whole is where they lost me. Sure, sure, I was guilty of crying, of searching for my Tom Cruise to complete, like I was the missing puzzle piece some dude was searching for. Until I realized that it was just romantic comedy bullshit and hardly a reality.

This romantic tale also provided me with another wicked life lesson I need to share.

Cuba Gooding Jr.'s character, Roy, has it right: SHOW ME THE MONEY! Roy is one of the football players Jerry is trying to get a kick-ass new contract for.

But my favorite aha moment is from when Roy gets injured on the field moments before he signs a new contract. He takes a brutal fall, which might end his career. He milks it, owns it, sits in it. In life, you will tumble. It's okay to stay down for a moment. Heck, enjoy the short-term attention, the "poor me" pity party. Sometimes, we aren't even that hurt, but we use every ounce of our being to secure an Oscar-worthy performance! You don't want to be taken off that field in a stretcher. You eventually wanna jump back up and run the field and slam that football into the ground. And make the crowd ROAR! Everyone likes a comeback kid, a warrior who overcomes injury or failure and takes life by the balls and gets that multimillion-dollar contract as the underdog!

Rescue your own damn self by knowing you complete you, boo, and no one else. Also remember to get yourself the fuck back up every time you fail or fall, and live sassily ever after!

Get Rid of the Skeletons in Your Closet!

I'm not talking about coming out of the closet sexually, although if now is your time . . . welcome, congrats, and make sure I'm invited to the party! I am talking about actually cleaning out your closet and getting rid of shit that has expired.

I get it; we have wicked clothes. We spend a ton of money on great fashion. But time after time, we hold onto items from ten years ago that are two sizes too small and taunt us on a daily basis. We anticipate the day we finally drop those last ten pounds and can zip up those jeans again!

I once owned a pair of size twenty-six Parasuco jeans. They cost me $200, which at the time was insane. They were the bomb. com! I think I fit into them one week before a fitness competition, and once when I had a brutal flu for ten days and couldn't eat. Every time I opened my closet, staring at me with their denim judgments and bitchiness were those perfect jeans that could not fit onto my "imperfect" body. Those jeans cried out to me, "Hey, you will never be good enough to ever wear me again!" *Well, fuck you, jeans!* I was an amazing size twenty-nine, but those jeans that I held on to with such high hopes and dreams kept me drowning in my sorrow. It was almost like I needed to prove the jeans wrong and become worthy enough to wear them again. One day, enough was enough. I donated them to the local shelter and replaced them with an equally amazing pair of True Religion jeans in size twenty-nine, which fit like a glove and gave me an ass that would rival JLo's. I walked into the local bar and the junk in my trunk was sassy for miles! I worked those jeans like a stripper works the pole!

Donating the nonsense that was holding me hostage, freed me. Don't let yourself be miserable over something in your closet. Life's too short to always be striving to fit into shit and being made to feel less than by denim.

 #storytime   **The Vegas Dress**

What piece of clothing haunts you? My client Lisa told me about a little black dress she had. Every single time she would have an event she would be on a quest to fit into that dress. The problem was, it never fit her in the first place. It was like she was remembering some dress that was supposed to fit like a size eight, but it fit more like a size two. She would cry for every event that she couldn't wear it to. A good friend's wedding was coming up and her ex, who we call "the fuckhead," was gonna be there with the girl he cheated on Lisa with. This meant we needed to call out the big guns! She showed up to one of our training sessions in tears. She did the dreaded closet-try-on that morning, and (of course) it still didn't fit.

"This is bullshit! Come to my closet. I want you to try on one of my forty-five little black slutty Vegas dresses I have in sizes eight to ten."

For those of you wondering what a slutty black Vegas dress is, it's a dress you legit can't wear anywhere else in the world or for anything other than being super drunk and in the casinos, shows, and bars in Las Vegas. You know, *the* dress. I told her I was sick of her closet and that damn dress. That dress sucked! She didn't suck!

Picture this: The day of her friend's wedding, Lisa walked in wearing a curve-hugging slutty, yet elegant, size eight dress of mine. She was radiating pure fierce, badass, sexy babe vibes. She had a smile on her face and fire in her eyes as she strutted her shit into that reception hall. And her shithead ex's face was full of regret as he realized his fuck-up. He was never getting that hotness again!

Moral of the story: Clean out your damn closet and fill it with clothes that make you feel amazing and actually fit. Wear things that make you feel fan-freakin'-tastic!

Rescue your own damn self from the madness of tight clothing that haunts you and makes you feel like shit, and live sassily ever after!

(PS: If anyone ever needs a slutty—I mean sexy!—Vegas dress to show their loser ex what they lost or to just rock a party, my closet is always open for you!)

Happy, Happy, Joy, Joy!

Happiness is an art. It's a practiced "thing" we need to dig deep to cultivate. It really is so much easier to sit in our sadness than it is to embrace being happy or to have joy. You see, most of us are scared to be truly happy for fear it's gonna just be taken away in an instant.

What is happiness? I like to think of happiness being like how a toddler is when they see their favorite toy! Or how a cat is when their owner comes home after being away at work for the day. Nope, I meant dogs. Cats are assholes! For me, happiness is a Chipotle burrito and a glass of Pinot Grigio (with ice!). #nojudgments #simplethings

Happiness looks different for everyone. Heck, it changes moment to moment, year to year, as we progress in our own lives.

How do you practice being happy more often? It just can't be as easy as saying, "Hey, I'm happy!" I realized it takes effort to be happy. But practice makes perfect. The last few years, I've committed to spending less time in the shadows of sadness and more time just being happy as fuck!

How did I do it?

The easiest thing I did was smile more. I get it; the world is a scary place. There is a lot to worry about, a lot to be sad about, and a lot of crap to deal with. But each morning, I start my day smiling at myself in the mirror. "Hey, baby girl, I see you, and today is gonna be a happy day!" I often remind myself to be happy, especially when sadness creeps back in. I also began spreading "Lori's SUPER smile." What the heck is this crazy lady talking about? It's smiling as much as I can and making eye contact when I do it with as many people as possible in a day. And no, not in the creepy Chucky doll (remember those?!) kinda way! I walk my dogs and make an effort to smile at each and every person I come into contact with. At the bank, entering shopping malls, heck, I smile at the car next to me when we are at red traffic lights. Sure, I may look like a weirdo to some, but for the most part, people smile back. Smiles are contagious.

Another free and easy way to gain more happiness? Compliment people as often as you can. Make it genuine, but make it happen. **The more you lift others up by telling them amazing things about themselves, the happier you will feel.** It always comes back full circle! My daughter, Brooklyn, is nineteen now, but ever since she could speak, I swear this was her thing. I remember being in a very busy grocery store when I noticed it first. She was around four years old. The cashier was slouched over with a sad look on her face, not making eye contact. She just looked miserable, like she might cry at any given moment. People were being idiots and mean, and it was just a draining environment. My daughter with her Shirley Temple curls blurted out, "Wow, you have the most beautiful eyes!" to the cashier. I have never seen someone's posture and expression change so quickly in my life. She thanked my daughter, then just carried on ringing through our groceries with a big smile on her face and light in her eyes. I thought this was a one-off until I started to watch my daughter interact more often with others as we ran errands. At the bank, she ran into a lady who seemed anxious. She was fidgeting and looked flustered. Brooklyn again made eye contact with her and said loudly, "Wow, you have such beautiful nails. I love that color on you!" She was so young, but she could feel that the woman needed more happiness. And in turn, it just gave her more bliss to lift others up. The woman slowed down, enough to stop and chat with my daughter. As she walked away, she carried herself with such a different energy—a better one. I learned from my daughter the happiness you get when you compliment others.

I often used to think happiness was an external thing, like vacations, diamonds, and money.

I used to believe happiness was marrying Idris Elba and running off to Bora Bora (actually that would make ME happy!).

In the end, happiness isn't about big items, it's more about the little things.

Flipping the switch from down to up.

Turning frowns upside down.

Taking a small moment to make someone else's day.

Being intentional with your words, thoughts, and actions. Everywhere you go. With everyone you meet.

Rescue your own damn self by sharing happiness and spreading more moments of joy with others, and live sassily ever after!

Block, Unfollow, Unfriend, and Mute Are a Girl's Best Friend!

....

My name is Lori, and I am sick of being *social* on social media!

The idea of gathering people online to check out what old boyfriends were doing or how fat they got was great on paper. Insert the insanity of filters, fakes, phonies, obsessions, lies, facades, addictions, feelings of less than, feelings of WTF, and I'm exhausted from social media. And it's not getting any easier to manage: Facebook, Instagram, Snap Twits, and Tic Chat (my teen is rolling his eyes at me. Mom, it's Twitter and SnapChat and TikTok, do I need to explain to you again what a "reel" is and why it's different from a story?!). I'm at my limit in terms of how social I ever wanted to be.

A lot of us do this little dance with the modern-day devil in disguise that helps us laugh at cute puppy videos one moment, then turn around and feel less than after scrolling the 'gram filled with filtered fitness influencers the next!

There is a movement for everything on there now. #bodypositive, #metoo, #timesup, #BLM, hashtags about anything, reels that make no sense and are about nothing, and endless stories about personal shit that should never be on the internet in the first place. It's a rat race of keeping up with the crowds on the newest platform of "look at me." Likes, follows, shares, friends, saves. I'm so dizzy, I'm spinning out of control!

⚘ #storytime Social Media Detox—The Only Cleanse I Will Do

Part 1: Block. Yep, this is something that will be your best friend after that breakup. You know, the one that caused you to cry so hard you lost all your false lash extensions your tech just applied the day before. That one true love who not only crushed your soul by sleeping with the neighbor, but now is parading that new love affair on their Facebook personal page. "Block!" I used to feel like I was being rude for bringing out this little button. Now, if you scroll my blocked list, you will find all the wrinkles and sleepless nights I've saved myself by just saying, "I never want to fuckin' see shit about that jerk again!"

Part 2: Unfollow. Post a video of someone hitting an animal or too much political jargon and it's a surefire way to end up in "unfollow" jail. I have this rule with social media now that if something is posted, even if it's my great-aunt Martha posting it, and if it brings up any negative vibes, feelings, or eye rolls, "unfollow" is my friend! I love that the other person also doesn't need to know I don't give a crap about every single moment of their lives enough to scroll endlessly or watch their breakdowns unravel. If it isn't serving me, I don't allow it to take up any space in my feed.

Part 3: Unfriend. I have a truth bomb I'm dropping: Just because you have 1,678 friends on Facebook doesn't mean they are really your friends. Gasp! At one point, I had the max friends Facebook allows. I can't even remember the number, something like 5,000. Random strangers who I wouldn't know if I passed on the street. Guys who were complete jerks and I would watch them post their constant changing of girlfriends or new sports cars. People who, if I was sick or needed someone to help me, wouldn't break a sweat for me. People who wouldn't help me if I was down. "Friends" who didn't even know my kids' names or favorite wine! Deal breaker! When I realized I could cleanse the "friends" list, I got the number down to a more realistic two hundred on Facebook. Two hundred people I actually wanted to see updates and posts from, and two hundred people who genuinely cared about what the heck was happening in my life too.

Part 4: Mute. We all have bad days. We all have meltdowns or moments of darkness. But to watch it unravel on massively public social media platforms is maddening. I get it; your dog died, your husband lost his job, and you gained ten pounds. Now, your news feed is filled with quotes about life sucking or memes about your problems being "too much." I like you enough that I will allow you to stay one of my "friends," but we "need to take a break!" I might unmute you when you crawl out of the depths of depression or when the election is finally over and I know you will be done with your political rants. Or when the pandemic has run its course and I don't have to read all the conspiracy theories you are posting. "Mute" is just a short break, gurl, I'm not breaking up with you for eternity.

Phew, like any cleanse or detox I've ever done, I think I should celebrate with wine afterward. #idontcleanse But pass the wine before I block you!

Rescue your own damn self by realizing that you control your own social media, those buttons exist for a reason so use 'em, and live sassily ever after!

Snow White and the Seven Dwarfs

An apple a day is supposed to keep the doctor away, but if laced with poison by your jealous stepmother queen, apples can be deadly.

Lori's *Fast and Furious* Fairy Tale Breakdown:

* Beautiful princess (always stunning, she's never frumpy with an overbite!) loses her father to death and of course, her new stepmother, **the queen**, is a jealous lunatic who has a warped relationship with a possessed mirror. She asks it if she's the prettiest one around and the mirror crushes her dreams with an honest: "Nope, your stepdaughter **Snow White** is winning that race."

* The queen orders her guards to take Snow White to the forest to kill her, but they can't do it, so they set her free and tell her never to return to that toxic castle filled with that crazy step mama!

※ In the forest, she meets **seven dwarfs** and goes home with them to become their maid and chef! Strange, but I guess they did kinda save her first by giving her a crib to crash in.

※ She meets a **handsome prince** in the forest (wow, déjà vu from almost every other fairy tale!).

※ The queen finds out (from her all-seeing, all-knowing mirror) that Snow White isn't really dead. The queen turns herself into an old homeless woman who meets Snow White in the forest and offers her a big, juicy apple that she has secretly poisoned. Snow White takes a bite of the apple and falls under a deep sleeping spell. Everyone thinks she's dead and puts her in a glass coffin. Why didn't anyone check for a pulse before sealing her in a see-through casket? More déjà vu. Sounds like Sleeping Beauty (a beautiful princess poisoned into a deep sleep who can only be awakened with the kiss of a handsome prince), although she has three fairies compared with Snow White's seven dwarfs.

※ Of course, the prince is wandering again in the forest, kisses her, a woman he barely knows (#getconsent), she wakes, falls in love with him, he rescues her, and they live happily ever after!

The Facade or Complete Insanity in a Nutshell:

* Just like in *Cinderella*, this is another story of a father who married an evil woman and died without a will, ensuring that his sweet daughter (good old Snow White) would get raked over the coals by her horrible stepmother. Plan ahead, Papa!
* Well, mirrors aren't magic, and if they were, I would give them more credit for not messing with our minds as much as they do already!
* Seven little men, randoms, and a young innocent girl just deciding to move in together? Please, ladies, don't do this!
* Another girl falling in love with a man she doesn't know, being saved by him, and being happy for life? Sure, sure! #thisisbull

Lori's Revamp of this Madness—*Snow White*, Take 2

* Snow White and the seven babes. Okay, more believable to me is that she is in the forest, stumbles upon seven kick-ass women who take her into their awesome house and build up her self-confidence enough so she knows NOT to talk to random old ladies,

much less eat apples from them! And she lives happily ever after with her besties by her side, no need for a man to save her!

✳ Snow White and the seven dwarfs go rogue. For ten years, she cleaned and cooked for them. Legit, what if before the queen came with the apple, she decided she was exhausted from slaving over that oven and the constant sweeping up after those seven annoying men. I mean, they sneeze and snore and are grumpy! Maybe let the girl sleep! Seven men would exhaust me! So, she packed her bags and saved her own damn self and headed for Vegas, where she won the jackpot and lived happily ever after!

✳ Queen gets an ego check and an education in the comparison game. Don't let the mirror play tricks with you! Asking the mirror who was fairest was setting the queen up for the jealousy game. Work on your self-esteem, sister! Looks aren't everything. Be the queen who makes a difference in the kingdom so no one is worried about who is the hottest. Look in that mirror and know you are the best *you* on the planet! Maybe she looks in the mirror, sees the terrible job she's doing as a step mama, brings Snow White back, and ends up being the cool grandma to her future grandkids. Let's find some self-love and acceptance and stop comparing our forty-five-year-old selves with nineteen-year-olds! Okay, I'm talking about myself now and the social media rat race, not just the evil queen!

Rescue your own damn self by knowing you can say no to the poisonous apple, open that bottle of Pinot Grigio instead, and live sassily ever after!

A Family Is What You Make It!

....

Boy meets girl, boy marries girl, they have two kids, a boy and a girl. That was considered a family. Grandma and Grandpa usually were still married and lived three houses down the street. Insert a dog or a cat, and there were the stick figures on the back window of their minivan.

The family!

Who remembers *The Brady Bunch*? I watched this show religiously as a kid. The awe of seeing a "not normal" family unit. Mom and Dad are remarried now, the woman had three girls, the man had three boys, and now the family unit looks very different. You see, I came from that typical "Mom, Dad, boy, girl, four-person family." Most of my friends growing up were also in that exact same family unit. Watching *The Brady Bunch* and seeing this unusual family that looked different and actually *worked* was so new to me. I found it fascinating.

Then as I grew up, I realized the world is a large place, and filled with diversity and differences. I started to look around and take in all the ways in which a family can look, beyond what we were told in the past. We evolved as a society, and we have embraced the "non-nuclear" (four-person family). It has radically changed.

A family is what you make it! No one else gets to tell you *who* will be your family. We surely don't have to fit that mold anymore.

Family that was once only defined as those to whom you are "related" genetically is now a thing of the past. Blood doesn't have to be in the equation at all. Love is!

Annie

This movie is on the top of my list for introducing me to the amazing concept of adoption. Not every adoption starts with a cute-faced sassy redhead and her dirty mutt. But the idea that a child can be brought into a family by choice and love rather than blood melts my heart. There are so many children in the world who are full of love to share and a desire to be accepted for who they are.

Flying solo

My client Elizabeth has never been married. The idea of marriage didn't fly with her. She came from a family that changed three times during her childhood and teen years. At the age of thirty, she decided that even though she could get pregnant herself, she would adopt. This was twenty-five years ago, so times have changed since then. No agency would give her a baby. She wasn't the nuclear family they were looking for on their application. Eventually, the world started to get their shit together and realize single parenting was a thing. Elizabeth has not one, not two, but three adopted children now. She has lots of love to give and a warm and safe space to raise her little family, alone! Divorce or death often turns a family into a single-parent household anyway. Elizabeth actively chose to rescue herself and create the life that she desired, in a way that felt good for her. Society's ideals be damned!

No kids, no problem

Couples without children are sometimes called "childless families." People used to be shunned for making the decision to "not have kids." It's more common now to see a family unit consisting of just a man and a woman, or a man and a man, or a woman and a woman.

The ugly stepmother

Fairy tales really cast stepmothers in a bad light! But in reality, with divorce rates through the roof, having stepparents is more common than you can imagine. In fact, it's now a norm that your family might be Mom and her new husband and his kids, just like *The Brady Bunch*. In the show, Mike was a widower, but Carol's ex was never mentioned. Divorce was such a taboo then that they didn't want viewers thinking about it. Now, blended families are seen on screen and in real life.

LGBTQIA2+ families

To me, love is love is love. Thankfully, the adoption world has evolved and opened up and for the most part, people are able to adopt children based on love and equal human rights, instead of their sexual orientation.

I don't have time or space to keep listing the many ways in which a family can be. Family isn't just a mom and a dad. It can be grandparents or other relatives raising children who aren't theirs. It can be multiple families living in a community within a home or commune. Regardless of what your family tree looks like, family is what you make it!

I consider my besties and their kids my family. I've lived far away from my family for decades, most of my whole life. So, my family unit includes anyone I love. If you are in my circle and special to me, you are my family! Not all of us are lucky enough to have living parents, our own children, a spouse or partner, so we embrace those who don't have a family into our family. My client Tina lives with two of her best friends. Three women. One of the ladies has two kids who also live with them. They are a family!

Rescue your own damn self by finding the family unit that works for you. Create your chosen family. Embrace that every family can look different and contain love, and live sassily ever after!

Stop Living in the False Promise of Tomorrow!

....

"When I lose ten pounds, I'm gonna look so much better!"

"When I am leaner, I am going to feel more secure and confident!"

"When I get X amount of money, I'm gonna stop the rat race!"

"When I finally find true love, life will be complete!"

When . . . When . . . When . . .

We wait for some false promise of happiness at the end of some rainbow like the pot of gold we might never find.

#truthbomb: We only get one life, and it goes quick. And it's short! Tomorrow is a gift that's not promised, earned, or guaranteed.

Every day, hundreds of thousands of people die. They take their last breath without knowing that it's actually going to be "the day." It's not marked on their calendar: die tomorrow! Harsh, but reality!

Someone who died this very second didn't know they were leaving us. The "see ya tomorrows" they said to their loved ones weren't true.

Life's too short to not be living for the moment, in the moment, like it might be your last moment.

 #storytime   **Remembering Vernon Marshall**

Five years ago, I was not living in the moment. I was living in the future, in the "five years from now." I opened Energy Fitness and Yoga, a massive fitness, yoga, and spin studio. The bills were insane. The workload was crazy. It was the most stressful time in my life. I owned a yoga studio, but I was a ball of nerves, anxiety, and constant depression. Yoga is supposed to bring balance and Zen, but I felt like I was digging my own grave. It was hell! #notkidding

My amazing friend Vernon was my shoulder to lean on. I would complain every day about not being happy, not feeling like this was what I wanted, not wanting to continue the madness. And in every single conversation he would say the same thing to me: "Life is too short, Lori, to be fuckin' miserable and not doing what you are meant to do."

I kept making excuses and justifying why I stayed. It was a lot of lost money if I closed (hundreds of thousands of dollars of my savings, not to mention my blood, sweat, and tears). But it was also the pride. The worry and fear of what people would think. I kept thinking that fear of being a "failure" would always haunt me. (Insert Lori's massive ego here!)

This madness continued for months and months (fifteen months to be exact!). I remember getting a text from Vernon trying to convince me to change: "Come downtown and visit, and close that fuckin' studio that is causing you gray hair and wrinkles, and come drink away the insanity and start living!"

I can remember as clear as day a few days later that same week. My phone rang just as I was getting ready to walk in to teach a yoga class at my studio. I was still miserable and stressed. It was a mutual friend of ours, and I could hear the crack in his voice like something was off. "Lori, sorry to tell you, but Vernon died yesterday!"

WHAM! That feeling of tons of bricks being thrown at you. That kick in the stomach!

I was completely paralyzed at that moment. Replaying that last text and knowing I hadn't done what he asked. I didn't get to see him downtown for fun, and I was still holding onto some ego trip I was on.

Vernon was young, fun-loving, and just living life. But almost to the point of living it too freely and making some choices with his life that eventually took him from us.

Like a robot, I hung up the phone and went to teach the yoga class. I was so distracted, and as my class members lay in savasana in silence, I sat cross-legged, holding back the overwhelming sadness and emptiness I was feeling. In that instant of complete quiet, I heard Vernon, just like he always had sounded: "If you aren't happy, fuck, girl, just quit already! Life is too short!"

The day I learned Vernon was gone was the same day I typed up the sign announcing to all my staff and members that I was closing down Energy Fitness and Yoga. I chose to put my happiness in top spot because I now knew that Vernon was right. Tomorrow isn't always promised to us. He sure didn't get any more days to keep living. He said goodbye to me and others a few days' prior, thinking he would be seeing us again. No one knows when their time is up. You might as well carpe diem the heck out of life and go after your dreams. Live a life that makes you happy!

I carry Vernon's advice with me every single day. I have chocolate when I want it. I love my body now, at this moment. Even with an extra bump, lump, or curve. I only do the things I enjoy doing. If I find something is weighing me down or not serving me, I cut ties with it quicker than I used to 'cause tomorrow isn't guaranteed.

Let go and apologize to someone you have wronged and were too pigheaded to admit it.

Let go of that grudge you have and offer forgiveness to someone who hurt you, just in case you don't get that breath tomorrow. That release feels so good.

Start each day with gratitude that you are thankful you are getting up again. Finish the day the same way, with thanks for having the day you had.

I have seen so much death and tragedy in my lifetime. But some of life's losses, like losing my amazing friend Vernon, have me always hearing his stern voice telling me that "life's too short to be miserable." And to remember that "the tomorrows are not always gonna be there so say it, do it, live it, today!"

Vernon couldn't be saved that day, but let's let his death remind us to make those harder choices now to ensure we're living like there might not be a tomorrow. RIP, V! xo

Rescue your own damn self by seizing the day, today, and live sassily ever after!

You Never Know What Is Happening Behind Closed Doors!

....

"Did you hear about Colin and Susie? They got a divorce!" (Gasp!) "I always thought they were the perfect couple!"

I swear I've heard that statement more times in my life than I'd like to admit.

That narrative we all have for other people's lives.

The romantic fairy tale we make up in our heads about that amazing couple, when in reality, it's an action-packed shitstorm behind closed doors.

Why do we do this? Why do we believe that everything we see on the outside is the entire happy storyline?

Boy meets girl, boy and girl fall in love, boy and girl are so damn happy and loving in front of everyone. But the girl is miserable and in a sexless marriage behind closed doors. Boy hates his life, has a drug problem, and both of them are one step away from a *Dateline* episode!

I always laugh at my friends when they say, "I thought they were so happy and in love!"

Yeah, and I thought Santa Claus was real because my parents told me this for most of my childhood, until I caught "Santa" putting out the presents and realized he was my dad.

Heck, we all thought Bill Cosby was dad of the year, not some sicko drugging innocent women's drinks and doing God knows what when they were passed out! Ya never really know people! #mrhuxtablewasabadman

Marriage, relationships, and love are freakin' hard! We know this!

Staying happy with the same person day after day, year after year in the stressors of life is impossible for most of us to sustain.

So, this idea of thinking we know the whole story of the "perfect couple" is utterly ridiculous.

The shock factor of a performance we all put on when we hear about a breakup or a relationship struggling is comical. No Oscar performances around here.

Sure, we sometimes get to see those happy and nostalgic times. Stress free, so much love, happiness.

But what we don't see is the behind-the-scenes footage. The bloopers, the scenes they want to be cut out of their performance.

We're human, and we don't want people to see the messy parts.

But everyone's shit stinks, and everyone's relationships will have their ups, downs, and sometimes, abrupt endings.

I had this friend who once found out her husband had gambled away their life savings. He was an alcoholic, and she didn't even know he was drinking again. He had been cheating on her for years. She would show up to parties smiling, talking about how amazing her husband was, how his job was going so well, and the trips they were planning. Not only did I not know of the struggles she was having, she didn't even know it. Because he was keeping it behind closed doors. When it all came out and their separation was "announced" to the public on social media, a shitstorm of people began sending me messages.

My response to these situations is always the same:

I hope she is okay. (Always my number one concern.)

Well, we never know what's happening behind closed doors.

Nothing ever shocks me. (Legit, I have seen it all in this lifetime!)

What I learned is that we never really know the full story unless it's our own. Heck, even if it's our own relationship, we don't always know all the sides of it. Look at my friend who didn't even know she wasn't in a happy relationship, free of gambling, addiction, and despair! We know our role in the stories of life, but we don't control the other characters. In fact, we haven't even read the full script! So nothing should shock us. What happens behind closed doors is often a big secret. That's the reality of life!

Rescue your own damn self by realizing it's okay to have shit happening that no one sees, it's okay to be shocked when you are still trying to believe someone out there has cracked the "perfect life" code, but own it knowing most of us have our own mess behind closed doors, and live sassily ever after!

Wedding Crashers and 27 Dresses . . . I Do!

"Do you take this man to be your lawfully wedded husband, Lori?"

"I DO!"

Insert waterworks, the crowd cheering, and bring on the happily ever after!

Who here loves a good wedding? Show of hands! ME!

I can show up to any wedding of any person, whether I know them or not, and CRY!

Are they happy tears? I would like to hope so. Sometimes, they're sad ones, though. Maybe it's the pessimist in me that looks at the sorry souls standing at the front of the altar thinking, *It's all love, and sunshine, and carefree times now! Wait for a year or two . . . or ten! Wait till they forget to put the toilet seat down and your ass falls clear into it at 2 a.m. for the final straw!*

Why is it so hard for me to just push that aside and think that everyone will live happily ever after?

Why does my mind need to wander to the current divorce rate and know that less than 60 percent will make it work?

Okay, I will take my super negative visions and bury them just for a moment, so that I can try to remember love. L-O-V-E, raw and stripped down, the feeling of butterflies in your stomach, the throbbing of your heart, knowing that your body and soul are connected to this other amazing human you are about to spend the rest of your life with.

Yep, I am still a hopeless romantic. That is why weddings make me cry. Because in that very moment, even if it's going to be short term and end in sadness, there is still that carefree, happy feeling of love that "this person is my everything." I still believe in L-O-V-E!

I couldn't choose just one movie to remind us of the plot of weddings and why we love them so much. And I actually don't want to change the storyline of these at all—no rewrites—instead, just a couple of life lessons and reminders:

Wedding Crashers—Vince Vaughn is . . . mmm, wait, what was I saying?

Quick rundown: Two crazy, cute friends crash weddings to pick up hot, desperate babes because usually we ladies are craving love and thinking *It could be me next.* Both guys meet women they actually DO love, end up with them, and live happily ever after, ending all of their skepticism of marriage.

So, they, too, are like me, always out for a good party, trying to have a good time, and are really not too sure about this whole "for life" scenario. But then . . . WHAM! Love still hits them hard!

My takeaway from this amazing romantic comedy is that **love is love**! Sure, we may find love and lose love, but there is still always more love. Love is everywhere! No, I haven't been smokin' anything! What I am trying to say is that we can't give up on the idea that love is replaceable and always around us and within us. We always have more love to give and receive. We never run out of it. I have learned this in my life. Broken hearts can be mended. Lost loves can be replaced with new loves. *Love is love*. It's not going anywhere. So, when you are at that next wedding watching the bride and groom, or groom and groom, or well, two people at the altar saying "I do," sob with happiness. Because on that day, it's the love we all have to hold onto that makes the world go round and reminds us it's such a good feeling to be lucky enough to have! **Don't lose the belief in L-O-V-E!**

Anyone need a date for a wedding? I need a good loco-motion train and some open bar kinda booze! I dance a wicked "Macarena!"

27 Dresses—Short recap of this movie: Girl is a bridesmaid in twenty-seven weddings, with all the ugly dresses to prove it. She's a love skeptic, but she meets a guy, falls for him, and gets to finally be a bride instead of a bridesmaid!

The amazing takeaway or life lesson from this movie is this:

You will get your turn. Patience, young Jedi! (*Star Wars*, anyone?)

I get it; we watch others around us find their prince or their life partner. Some of us just have to wait our turn longer! Sit on the sidelines of the field and cheer on our friends first! In my life, I really believe that **love finds you when you are ready, willing, and able!** We need to take a deep breath and make sure when it does come, we've got wide open arms ready to snap it up!

There have been times in my life when I met someone special, and I was in a mental shitshow state. There was no way I loved myself, much less had the ability to receive it from someone else. Timing is everything in love. When we are truly ready, it is there. So being that bridesmaid and supporting your friends as they find love doesn't mean you won't ever get "your turn." Your turn is coming, and when it does, your friends will be celebrating you.

#truthbomb: Facial expressions are worth a million dollars on that big day. Wait for it . . . duh, duh, duh, duh . . . that moment the bride is about to walk down the aisle. And just as the groom (or partner at the other end waiting) catches a glimpse of her, it's that look he gives. His eyes, his smirk, maybe it's his tears (I've seen my share of sobbing grooms). *That* right there is the moment you feel the love. You feel that deep connection, that chemistry. The skeptic in you disappears, and in that instant, you might be thankful you've already found that with someone, or you can be optimistic that you, too, will find it one day!

If you have lost love through divorce or death, try going to someone's second wedding. There's something powerful about finding love later in life. We are more mature and know what we want. We know what didn't work during our first go-round, and we've learned more about ourselves and what we can give and take in love. It's a whole other dimension of believing that *love is love* and there is always more love coming! Unlimited supply chains of L-O-V-E!

Love is everywhere. Although it feels like it leaves us, don't lose the belief that you can and will always find it! With each version of ourselves in our evolution, our growth, our quest for love, we will find a love that matches our best selves. Rescue your own damn self from your disbelief in the L-word, and live sassily ever after!

Hormonal Hell Exists!

....

Okay, you are busting your ass in the gym and are laser-focused on nutrition. You're counting calories, measuring every morsel of food, and are really focusing on your "plan." You are working your ass off, but your body isn't changing or responding. In fact, you've got a new spare tire around your waist, but you're not a car! No matter what lengths you go to, you can't lose weight and are in fact gaining it! You tear up when you see puppies on the street. You get distracted more easily in traffic or break down when something minor doesn't go your way. You find yourself wanting to scream into a pillow most of the day over the smallest missteps, and it constantly feels like you're a bloated, sweaty hot mess! Welcome to hormonal hell!

Hormones, everyone has 'em! They build bones, maintain muscle, and do other amazing things for the body. But if they're out of whack, they can be a recipe for disaster. Hormones play a huge role in how we age, grow, and function, and when out of sync or imbalanced, it's a shitstorm of insanity! Raging hormones can take us from acting like Glinda the Good Witch to a raging fire-breathing dragon at the drop of a hat!

No one teaches us this in school. "Hey, Emma, when you hit

thirteen, you will be crying and sobbing hysterically and won't understand why. Hormones!"

 #storytime   **Iced Caps Cause Meltdowns**

Six years ago, my daughter turned thirteen, and that was when I realized that teenage (and puberty) hormones were serious shit! I woke her up for school one day, just like the usual morning, and she came out of her room to ask me if we could stop at the local coffee shop on the way to school to get her friend an iced cappuccino for her birthday. I had a busy day ahead and declined her request nicely. Little did I know that shit was about to hit the fan. Cue the hormonal frenzy. She began sobbing and having a panic attack and curled into a ball in the corner screaming, "Whyyy?" I swear my neighbors must have alerted the authorities over her tantrum. This emotional breakdown continued for thirty minutes. At one point, she even admitted to not knowing why she was even crying. I had to load her, possibly toss her, in the car to get her to school for the day. She continued to sob the whole way. Upon arrival at the front loop of her high school, the car went quiet. She opened the car door, turned and smiled at me and said, "Bye, Mom, have a good day, see you later!" And just like that, the meltdown was a distant memory. Like it hadn't happened. Like that was a different personality! I was flabbergasted. Couldn't even explain it until I realized . . . hormones!

No one teaches us that after this pubescent hormonal shift, we also hit a pre-midlife one. "Hey, Cathy, when you hit thirty-five you are going to start gaining weight rapidly, your periods will be so heavy you can't leave the house, and you will probably break out in night sweats!" No one tells us this shit! We have to be in the deep end of the pool drowning to realize something ain't right!

My client Donna once texted me from the gym: "My period is killing me. I'm bleeding so much that I'm about to sprint on the treadmill and my uterus might just fall out!" We laughed, but it's serious shit!

Perimenopause is the preshow to the main event of menopause (which I wrongly assumed only affected older women). Nobody ever told me perimenopause can start as soon as your early thirties. So, when I started to gain weight, had insane mood swings, hot flashes, was crying for no reason, had night sweats and boobs so sore I couldn't sleep, I realized something was off. It was almost impossible to rescue myself from anything when I was a big, fat, hormonal, shitstorm of emotional messiness! I was not in control of any dragon slaying or life living! No diet regimen, no workout routine, no amount of suffering could help me get that killer physique I was after. Heck, I was just having a hard enough time functioning day-to-day just being in my body, much less rescuing myself from anything! Some days I didn't want to have a life, and I started to hate everyone around me.

Hormonal swings can be so dramatic and cause such batshit extremes that some women have committed major crimes (a.k.a. murder or mutilation) from their whacked-out imbalance, then used that as their defense. It's serious shit! Don't let yours get out of control, and don't go chopping off penises, even if ya wanna! "It wasn't me, Officer, it was my hormones."

Heck, don't let them affect your happiness and your day-to-day life. That's no way to live. We need to see doctors, and when they say we are "normal" and "fine," we need to see naturopaths, holistic practitioners, and acupuncturists, anyone who can help us find supplements, medications, or natural remedies to not feel like such garbage. Sure, hormones are a part of life, but let's try to keep them somewhat balanced to help the quality of it. Google "hormones are pissing me off," join a health program, do whatever is needed. Join women's health and wellness support groups full of other estrogen-surging maniacs trying to find balance. Do what you need to do!

Rescue your own damn self by learning that hormonal hell is a real thing, and once we can get the old hormones working like a well-oiled car, we can live sassily ever after!

If It Sounds Stupid, It Is!

....

If it sounds too good to be true, it usually is. I remember being told this as a child. Or if something sounded "too easy," it meant it was really hard and that it would bite me in the ass later for thinking it would be a piece of cake.

If it sounds stupid, looks stupid, acts stupid, and your gut tells you it's kinda stupid, then it probably IS stupid!

Working in the fitness industry for thirty years, I have seen it all. False claims, empty promises, magic pills, insane solutions with crazy rebounds. Foul-tasting concoctions and torturous contraptions. Endless madness!

If you aren't born with a small waist, buy this amazing "waist-trainer" and you will get two inches off your waist in only months of use! #bullshit

Hmm, that sounds stupid, number one; legit, sounds painful, number two; and sounds impossible and ridiculous, number three. Sign me up!

Repeat after me: some torture device isn't going to change my shape by altering the waist and body I was born with. It's a bullshit solution!

If you wanted your feet smaller, you wouldn't cut off your toes to make it happen. You just need to research foot binding to see how such a horrible and debilitating act can ruin lives.

The same applies to the promise of waist shrinkage. It's dangerous because it moves your internal organs around and does permanent damage, yet women still search for these products and believe the ridiculous promises. Don't ignore my life lesson of "if it sounds stupid—training your waist to just shrink—then it is stupid!"

Two decades ago, one of my best friends at the time bought a corset ("waist-trainers" weren't a thing back then, but really, they're the same thing). She wore it religiously for months and months. She had bruises along the sides of her waistline from the endless hours she sported it. She assumed she had to wear it 24/7 and didn't sleep because of discomfort. We measured weekly. And do you want to know what happened in the six months of wearing it? Not a damn thing! Not any change! Nada! Another friend did the same little science experiment and lost a half inch (that's it!), and within a few days of not wearing it, her waist went back to where it was before—a half inch bigger!

Fad diets are another "stupid is as stupid does" (*Forrest Gump*, anyone?) trend for us all to be aware of. They usually have special (and weird) rules for cutting out entire food groups and taking secret pills or solutions. The lists are endless.

Hands up? Ever try a fad diet? How was it? Did you see the

promised overnight results? Did you keep those "promised" results for the long term? Are you still doing this same diet now? Did you kill anyone while doing the diet? #ithappens

Fad diets often become popular quickly, like some cult promising dramatic results (usually in the fastest time possible to keep everyone's attention span) before the next fad can take its place. Fads are never sustainable and can often cause physical or mental damage for the long term. Even if they do work in the short term, they're only a bandage solution that usually results in a big-time rebound.

I've researched countless fad diets in my career, and I can't believe the stupidity we've bought into through the years! From liquid diets to protein-only diets, from raw diets to maple syrup and cayenne cleanses, we've desperately searched for the quick fix, regardless of how awful it tasted or how disgusting it made us feel.

I won't turn this into a fad diet manual or a workbook on the stupid shit to avoid in the fitness industry. That's for another book entirely.

The moral of this epic adventure: rescue your own damn self by knowing that when it sounds silly, crazy, unreal, or stupid, IT IS, and live sassily ever after!

Ride the Wave, Dude!

Life is filled with ebbs and flows!

I don't surf. I tried once, but I couldn't even get myself into an upright position. That shit is harder than it looks! But let's roll with this as a metaphor for life.

If you finally do get lucky enough to get up on that surfboard and start riding the wave, you can't get off mid-wave or you will crash and possibly drown. You keep riding the wave until you conquer it. You keep on the path. If that wave doesn't work, there's always another one right behind it.

Surfers, who have conquered the giant wave that everyone else fears, know how it feels to be on top. To own it. To dominate it!

When a surfer crashes and burns (well, more like crashes and swims), they get back up on that board and ride again. In life, we can't get off the elevator between floors, and we shouldn't stop riding our "wave" for fear of crashing.

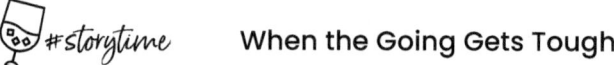 #storytime   **When the Going Gets Tough**

Picture it: You're in a new relationship. Life is good. Love is in the air. Juices are flowing, magic is happening, butterflies are having a party in your stomach! Then . . . WHAM! You're hit with that moment when you remember past heartbreaks, lost loves, terrible breakups. You get scared. You want to abort the mission, run, hide, and protect your heart. But you're torn because this is feeling pretty damn good. *What if this is the love of a lifetime? What if this one does work out?* What if you just stayed riding this wave to see how amazing it could be? Jumping off mid-wave means you'll come crashing down. So, ride it out and see what happens!

The same can be said for long-term relationships. My friend Katherine once invested nine years trying to be with someone she viewed as her soul mate. Nine years of ups and downs, rising and falling, short hellos and quick goodbyes, hot sex, then sexual droughts! Nine years of stress, anguish, and long-distance love, and never truly being able to be together. Just as she was about to pack it in, another friend said, "Katherine, ride the wave!"

At the time, I rolled my eyes and assumed we had all had too much Pinot Grigio! Then she explained, "For nine years, you've committed to finally being able to put your heart and soul into this love. If you stop now, you are getting off mid-wave. Life gets hard, relationships get hard, but you have never really gotten to give this one a full chance. If you get off the wave now, you're missing out on what could end up being the most amazing ride of your life! So, girl, get the heck back up on the surfboard and conquer that wave!"

Katherine rode that wave, and this year, she and her partner happily celebrated under a gazebo in front of friends and family as they said, "I do!"

Rescue your own damn self by riding that surfboard of life, and live sassily ever after!

Humpty Dumpty

Let's branch out here a little and head from Fairy Tale Facades to Nursery Rhyme Lessons and Lori's Sassy Rhyme Spinoffs.

"Do the Humpty hump—" Nope, that's a rap . . . let's recap this story from my youth.

Lori's *Fast and Furious* Fairy Tale Breakdown:

* An **Egg** sits on a wall (did no one see Michael Jackson dangling his baby off the balcony? This isn't a good idea, like legit!).
* Egg falls off the wall and of course cracks! #sawthatcoming
* All the king's horses and men can't repair him! Wait! Hold up, sista! What the heck? That is the end?! How hard did these people try? Didn't anyone have crazy glue or Scotch tape?

This is like a bad Netflix crime drama about a psycho serial killer that ends without anyone being caught or without any idea of who did it. That's it, goodnight. Like what the actual fuck?! I don't get closure? Or an explanation? Or a happy ending?

The Facade or Complete Insanity in a Nutshell:

* Why is an egg, clearly not a stable person, sitting on a high wall? It's round! I mean, I can kinda foreshadow what's about to happen here!
* No one, no doctor or nurse or handyman or contractor in the entire kingdom, could put him back together? Really?

Lori's Revamp of this Madness—
Humpty Dumpty, Take 2

I'm gonna play devil's advocate here and speak from the experience of being "broken" many times. I can kinda feel for good old Humpty!

Plot Twist #1—It's okay to break into pieces sometimes! Maybe he was on the wall at his breaking point (no, not suicide). Maybe it was his rock bottom. Maybe in falling off that wall and breaking down completely, he could then rise back up, putting the pieces together himself. Maybe falling off that wall meant he could rebuild in a new way, not "same-same!" In my life, I fell during my lowest of the lows. I stayed broken for a while. And when I did get back up, I was a different person. A stronger and wiser badass babe!

Plot Twist #2—Smash to pieces and call your girls! Fall off that cute little ledge, then have your bestie show up, scoop up your pieces (I can't count how many times my bestie has had to pick me up off the floor, completely broken!), and head to the plastic surgeon to get bigger boobs and more Botox! Oh, this storyline is getting good!

Don't wait for those king's horses and men to put you back together! Rescue your own damn self by falling apart and putting your own pieces back where you want them. Or heck, stay broken for a while (#nojudgments), and live sassily ever after!

If You Altered It, Own It!

Hey, I am all about preaching realness, and to those who follow or know me, I am the first to be as real AF on all things that I say and do. But here's a little not-so-secret secret. I'm about 60 percent real and 40 percent fake. The things I post are 100 percent me, 100 percent my thoughts. But externally, I'm gonna tell ya, I'm not this perfect being you see on social media or standing in front of you! My boobs are fake, my lashes are fake, I get Botox, I have filler, my hair color is not natural (in fact, I've been dyeing it since I was a teen, so I'm not even sure what my real color is!).

I applaud anyone who wants to change something about themselves, and with cutting-edge technology and inventions, we can. But let's be honest with ourselves and those around us by owning it!

Let's spill the beans to other hot babes!

Let's admit it! Let the cat outta the bag!

Let's share our stories and experiences with others so they know the whole story and can decide for themselves what they want, need, or heck, what they don't want.

Let's realize that the more we talk about these things and normalize them, the more we can all rescue ourselves from thinking that life is "natural perfection."

Part 1: Hair color. When I was fourteen years old, I took my little blooming self to the local hairdresser and took the plunge. This was the first moment I was about to be a little fake, a little more made up. A little edgier, so to speak. I was born with this mousy, dirty blonde, kind-of-boring hair. And it was so freakin' curly that it looked like a dirty mop most days. I remember getting blonde streaks throughout the '80s. It was 1989, and we were about to hit the '90s when hairstyles were "go big and ridiculous" or go home! I've been every color in the book since then. Red, black, multiple shades of brown, every bleached shade of blonde, as well as blue, green, purple, and even neon pink and magenta. I had rainbow unicorn hair at one time too! The main point of sharing this is that it's okay to want to switch things up. It's okay to want to be a blonde if you were born a brunette or to color your hair every color imaginable, especially if it makes you feel confident, bold, free, sexy, and expressive.

Part 2: Lash extensions. This is the latest craze, and I have to say, I would rather cut off my left arm than forgo my lash extensions. #vanity Maybe a slight exaggeration, but I've seen myself without lashes, and it ain't a good look. I once had an allergic reaction to the glue and had to get them taken off, and let's just say, I resembled an alien from another planet during that time or Gollum from *Lord of the Rings*! When I got them back on, life felt complete. Heck, I went from a hot mess to a hot goddess! I can't live without my fake lashes, but I'm willing to admit my problem: "My name is Lori, and I have a lash addiction. It has been zero days without lashes." Does it make me less real, less natural? Sure, but again, it's all external, and I'm happy to shout the news from the rooftops with friends that lashes are life.

Part 3: Botox and fillers. This isn't going to be a "Botox-and-Fillers-for-Dummies" course. I am not going into the lengthy science behind what they are, what they do, and how they work, but I will give a simple rundown. Botox relaxes the muscles in the face, getting rid of that resting bitch face #rbf we all know and love. Or possibly giving you a meaner bitch face. It stops the ability to show people how pissed off you are when you are truly pissed off. Almost like Jedi-mind powers and keeps everyone around you guessing. Fun, right?! It takes those squint lines you got from sunbathing in the '90s with no sunscreen and smooths them out. It takes you from looking forty and tired to thirty and without children. "Lori, you look so rested," is always the type of comment I get when my Botox kicks in. It just makes me look "refreshed" and like I just got back from the spa, all Zen-like! Fillers smooth out wrinkles, too, but by putting a little plump-ness back in areas that are starting to lose their suppleness. I have always been an open book when it comes to this because much like filters and Photoshop on social media, I just don't think it's fair to other women to sell a version of yourself as being real when you've used these two things to alter your appearance. Own that shit! No judgments whatsoever. It's empowering to put it all out there and let others know that we are all aging. Some of us age more gracefully than others, but in the end, most of us just want it to slow the fuck down!

Part 4: Plastic surgery. Boob jobs, va-jay-jays, lipo, tummy tucks, butt implants. Are you buckled in for this one? I love seeing a celebrity pretend to be totally real—"I would never feel the need for plastic surgery!"—but when you scan back to pics of them a decade ago, they've got a different nose, lower cheekbones, and more junk in the front end. Just admit it. I'm going to lay it all out there for you goddesses. I used to be as flat-chested as a pre-teen boy! Flatter than flat. So, when I was able to afford it, I went under the knife. I actually don't look like I got breast implants and often people will argue with me over it and not believe me. Either that was money well spent or not, who knows. What I do know is that it helped with my confidence on so many levels. At the time, I taught aerobics classes at a local women-only health club. When I was about to go for surgery, I told all the members what was going to happen. It wasn't super common to talk about plastic surgery at all back then, but I wanted to put it out there so everyone knew and could ask me questions. I mean, I was about to leave spin class one week flat as heck and come back a week later with knockers spilling over my sports bra! They aren't bad detectives; they would have known. It would have been so obvious, and while I am all about shock value and bold moves, I knew that talking about it would open up space for any woman to ask me questions they might have been too afraid to before. I was the fake-tit whisperer, demystifying the taboo that surrounded all cosmetic enhancements and surgeries. I was spilling the deets and my boobs for all to see!

Whether it's a simple salon appointment to dye your gray hair or a six-hour surgery to make your boobs bigger, the more we normalize this type of conversation, the more educated we can all become. Because to me, being real is all about being honest when you aren't "real."

Remember the famous makeup slogan: *Maybe she's born with it. Maybe it's Maybelline?* Yeah, nine times out of ten, it is the Maybelline, my friends!

Rescue your own damn self by fessing up when you aren't born with it, when you altered it, enhanced it, lifted it, or tucked it, and live sassily ever after!

Rock Bottom Can Keep Going Deeper! Part One

Rock bottoms can come in various forms for all of us. No one is immune to them.

Rock bottom could come to us in the form of the death of someone we love.

It could be with the loss of a great love we thought would last for life in a breakup!

It could be a job loss or a business failure.

Rock bottom could come to us in financial struggles to buy food or pay the bills.

In all that tragedy and loss, it was the tougher times that truly helped us to soul search.

Learn.

Grow.

Evolve.

Pivot.

Then, after we have that "Oh right, that's it" moment, we can take that upswing. But that's our next chapter, our Part Two. This one is all about finding that rock bottom and waiting for that precious climb back up to the top before realizing, nope, rock bottoms can keep repeating. You sometimes don't get that rainbow in between storms. **Sometimes, rock bottom doesn't really have a "bottom" at all!**

Little secret to rock bottoms as well, it sometimes takes longer than you think to find your way back up. It's not always overnight; in fact, it rarely is!

Disclaimer: I didn't change the names in this chapter as most of my social media friends and family have seen me ugly cry over the loss of Baby Daniel and the heartbreak of his mama, one of my besties, Sandy. Even writing this chapter has me wanting to run and hug dear Sandy.

One of my best friends has had her share of struggles. Sandy was pregnant with her second baby. I can remember the day as clearly as when it happened eighteen years ago. She came home from her ultrasound, and as I bumped into her in the underground parking lot of the building where we both rented condos, I could see the look of utter despair in her tear-filled, swollen eyes. "The baby has a heart condition, and the doctors told me he won't make it, and to abort the pregnancy!"

Don't worry, Sandy decided to beat the odds and keep the baby. She took that risk and had her son, Daniel. Doctors had to perform numerous heart surgeries throughout "Baby Daniel's" life (even at eighteen years old, he was still Baby Daniel to me!).

This mama had her rock bottom that day she was told to not

have the baby. But that's when she also had an aha moment. Life tosses us things. She reminded me that God (Universe or whatever you believe in) does have plans, even when we don't understand them. This was dealt to her, and she would see how it all played out. If that meant one year with her new baby, great. If it meant the potential for a lifetime, then she was willing to gamble on heartbreak and take that chance.

You would think this was the only rock bottom this amazing soul would have to endure. Hardly!

A divorce from her husband Warren (who had his own battles), then the loss of his life by suicide seventeen years after that first rock bottom moment in the underground parking garage. Sandy (now a single mother to four children) was left alone. She had to parent, to sit at rock bottom, and to try and pivot. You would think that was her rock bottom—it had to be time to rocket back up to the top, right?! Life usually taught the lessons, then it was time for the upswing. Think again.

One year after Warren took his own life, Baby Daniel (now almost eighteen), went in for his scheduled heart surgery (as the body grows, the valves need replacing to also get bigger). This was a standard and routine surgery. For two months post-surgery, that rock bottom continued as Daniel battled for his life. He was in and out of hospitals, struggling to overcome infections, and was even airlifted to a hospital in another city. Rock bottom couldn't get any deeper now! For two months, this single mama struggled with not only juggling her other three children on her own, but by also trying to hold on to what little bit of positive spirit she could. She was sure this was just a hiccup or a bump in Daniel's road to recovery.

On Christmas Day, 2020, Heaven (or whatever perfect, magical place you believe in) got another amazing soul, as Sandy had to make the decision no mother should ever have to make. She had to decide to let Daniel go. With all the complications, seizures, and then a coma, Daniel suffered brain trauma. It was time for him to leave us in body, like he had in mind. Rock fuckin' bottom! I don't wish the loss of a child on my worst enemy, much less one of my best friends who just deserved a fuckin' break already!

You see, rock bottom seems to have many floors, many tiers, many levels, multiple events or tragedies. But in every stage, we learn, suffer, grow, evolve, and handle it. Life sucks ass sometimes—there is no other way to put it! I sat on that Christmas Day hating the world! How dare it give her that child to love and nurture for eighteen years! How dare it take him away from his siblings who had already lost their father so tragically just a year prior. FUCK THIS WORLD!

Then I realized that this was my life lesson. That at rock bottom, there can still be a rock bottom-er. Then it can keep going to rock bottom-est. Then, just as you think it's gotta be time for that lesson, that freakin' upswing, we find rock bottom-to-infinity-and-beyond! (*Toy Story*, anyone?)

Where I am going with this lesson is that my amazing friend Sandy still hasn't gotten to see the silver lining after that insane storm, or multiple storms! But she is stronger, she is here, she is a wonderful mama to her other three amazing kids. And SHE didn't break! She's got this! I have to believe that through all that sorrow, the good times are coming. Will there be another rock bottom? Absolutely. Will she take that rock bottom by the balls and say "bring it on"—and make it through? You better fuckin' believe it!

RIP, Baby Daniel. I love you, my sweet friend. Say hi to Warren for me. I know you are taking good care of your dad up there, and I promise your mom is taking care of me down here, even though it should be me taking care of her. Your mom is the strongest woman I know! I love you! xoxo

Rescue your own damn self when life throws you to rock bottom again and again, and live sassily ever after!

Rock Bottom Is Where We Learn the Epic Shit! Part Two

....

Tragedy to triumph.

Struggles to successes.

Breakdowns to breakthroughs.

Chaos to calm.

Failures to comebacks.

None of the *there's always a silver lining* made me feel better as I sat in the depths of utter despair and sorrow.

I used to see the struggles, failures, and life's messes as negative, sad, terrible, awful, and pathetic!

Remember the Daniel story? *FUCK THE WORLD* was my mentality when we lost that precious soul!

What could rock bottoms really freakin' be teaching us besides the fact the world isn't fuckin' fair?!

But the life lesson I got from all the insanity life tosses at me that kept my head under water screaming "why me!" is this:

Lori's life lesson—that massive aha moment—always happened as I sat in all those deep, dark holes of "rock bottom." Not as I propelled back up, or as I sat at the top!

The real wicked stuff happens when you sit down there at the bottom.

Someone who has never had the bad or hard times often takes for granted the times it is easy or amazing.

If we haven't had that terrible relationship that challenged us, we can't have a healthy one to know what we need and expect. Or deserve.

If we haven't had to hustle for the dolla' bills, we often take for granted when we have that cash flowin'!

When you are truly hungry, you appreciate a hearty meal a whole lot more than if you're always at the buffet your entire life.

In death or loss of someone, we often are reminded to smarten up and appreciate those who are still here with us!

My dad used to work all day at his nine-to-five job, then have to hustle and wash cars at the local Chrysler car dealership my uncle managed. He would take me with him and give me money for the bottles of soda from the pop machine (oh goodness, I'm old!).

We didn't have a lot of money. We relied on the baby bonus checks (a.k.a. the government check that came in the mail for families so they wouldn't starve!). We didn't have lavish things. We had to run our car into the ground before we got a new one. So, when we got shiny new wheels, it was awesome, and we cherished it. In not having lots of money growing up, I now can appreciate what that struggle was. So, when I do have money, you better believe I cherish the heck out of that and am thankful!

 #storytime

Lacey Loses It and Gains It in Rock Bottom

My friend Lacey was in love. This was it! Put a ring on it! Say I do. Shit! Nope, back up, annul it, this is NOT the one! She sat in complete sorrow. Forty thousand freakin' dollars spent on the wedding, all now her debt. No home, no spouse, and even her parents and family were disappointed in her complete "failure." Lacey tried to take her own life. Thank God she did a really shitty job and failed at that too! When I went to see her in the hospital, it was the moment I saw that that rock bottom had taught her a lesson. She was still here! Through all of that, she was still standing, or lying, in that hospital bed. The loss of love, money, family, even trying to end it herself led to her still lying there! Rock bottom showed her she was okay. She needed to keep pushing.

This story makes me believe that even in the depths of complete bullshittery, she took that rock bottom and made vodka lemonade! Wait, no, that's another chapter! Lacey made rock bottom her bitch!

Lacey left that hospital. She got a wicked promotion from work. The same work where she met Jamie. They bought the most amazing downtown condo. They didn't get married but lived together in love. She didn't speak to her family again because of the complete abuse they gave her after the breakdown of her marriage and their lack of support when she hit rock bottom. But

Jamie's family was loving and supportive and took her in as one of their own. Will she have another rock bottom? Maybe, but if you ask her, she'll say this: "Well, I had one before, and I am here, so fuckin' bring it on!"

Rescue your own damn self by learning that rock bottom is your biggest teacher if you can wipe the tears, stop screaming why, and just listen to what the heck the Universe is trying to teach you, and live sassily ever after!

Sleepless in Seattle

Ladies, please do not meet a man on the internet or some radio show you listen to and fall madly in love with whatever crap you were sold. Please also don't meet this "random" at the top of the Empire State Building, ALONE! Legit, make smart choices! #strangerdanger

Okay, this movie hit me hard back in the day, that is until I became a mother. Until I began my addiction to crime shows, especially *Dateline*, *Law & Order*, and *Criminal Minds*. I realized *Sleepless in Seattle* makes no sense, and I really need to advise against it! Or rewrite it.

We're in the day and age now where we online date and meet people on social media. In today's world, we often have relationships with people before we even meet them face-to-face! It's the era of dick pics when we least expect them or didn't ask for them! #warnagal

While I love that this allows us to connect with people and shop around for what we like and don't like, hello, safety first, always!

The facade of profiles. You see, people can say anything, post any pic, claim to be anyone, and just make shit up! The world is filled with filters, Photoshop, and fake people. So, please have your guard always on high alert! This after-school special was brought to you by Starbucks! (Yep, I am still holding out for that sponsorship!)

Premise of the movie for those who haven't seen it:
- Annie (Meg Ryan) hears about widower and single dad Sam (Tom Hanks) on a radio show when his son calls in to find his dad a new love. He wants him to be happy. She legit doesn't know anything about him and if there is even passion or connection. I mean, it's a radio show!
- She's even engaged to someone else, but from just a few phone calls with this new random stranger, she is smitten!
- She goes all the way to the Empire State Building to meet him (BY HERSELF!). They meet, fall madly in love, and as they walk away and the credits roll, we are to assume they live happily ever after!

Now, this worked because it was Tom Hanks she got to meet at the top. It could very well have ended up being Ted Bundy or Charles Manson! Seriously, smarten up, ladies!

I get that we often won't find love the old-fashioned way of meeting a guy at the gym or at the local grocery store or through friends, so online dating is a thing. I am a dinosaur and a skeptic and far too cynical to think my soul mate is online just 'cause his dating profile pic claims to be him!

I have a better plot twist for this one.

- Girl meets guy's cute kid on some radio show. It's so awesome that he wants love for his widower dad.
- Girl talks to the guy. He's nice.
- Girl does a background check, stalks this guy for a while, then with her best friend in tow, she meets him in a public café (and ensures this isn't a future *Dateline* episode about the search for her dead body!).
- They like one another and date for a while, but they realize they aren't soul mates and end up with two other people after later swiping right.

Oh, Lori, you know you want to believe that sometimes good old romance means maybe it just works out.

Remember that safety comes first in your quest to find your special someone to rescue your own damn self with, and live sassily ever after!

Sidenote: This warning goes for online dating as well. Just 'cause the guy on Tinder says he's rich, smart, and cool, only meet him in a public and busy location for the first five to ten dates, and for goodness' sake, Google is your friend! I can legit find out someone's full history and shoe size with my detective skills on the internet!

Sharing Appetizers Trumps a Lonely Entrée Any Day!

....

You are out for dinner and drinks with your bestie. You order the chicken salad, and when the entrées come, you glance over at her fish tacos and think, *Dang! I should have ordered that!*

Life is so much more exciting when we get to try a bunch of stuff.

Life is so much better when we can have variety.

Life is complete when you can go out with your bestie and instead of getting the boring single entrée, she turns to you and says, "You wanna split like five different appies?"

#storytime Cactus Club Is My Jam— A Culinary Adventure

Where I live there is a restaurant chain called Cactus Club Café. By mentioning them I am hoping they will want to sponsor me since those who know and love me know I'm obsessed with this place. I enjoy routine, and I rarely go anywhere else to dine.

"Lori, wanna meet for drinks and appies?"

My response will always be, "Yep, which Cactus Club location?"

Pinot Grigio with ice (fo' sure!) and of course nine ounces, 'cause who in the heck gets six ounces, like really? I mean, just bring the bottle to save yourself some time and energy!

- Tuna Stack
- Ravioli and Prawn Trio (but bring four because I don't share well!)
- Szechuan Chicken Lettuce Wraps
- Mini Crispy Chicken Sandwiches
- Crispy Yam Fries with garlic aioli ('cause hello, yam fries are my jam)
- I can list another ten appies I would be happy to share here; they are all amazing!

Don't get me wrong, the lesson here is for sure that life is more fun when we can share with others! The real takeaway is that by coming together, allowing ourselves to flow in the moment and share our experiences with each other, we get to try a variety of things.

#storytime   **Variety Is the Spice of Life**

My friend Kristy was once on a first date with a guy she met on Bumble (how does anyone keep all these dating apps straight?). They went to a local hot spot for dinner and drinks. She texted me after and said, "I will marry this man! He asked if we could share a bunch of appetizers, and he now has my heart for life!" Legit, a fella who just met you and wants to share a variety of kick-ass food, shows he is all about teamwork, unafraid to share, and committed to your satisfaction for variety! Put a ring on that one! Kristy and I often had the conversation about "the entrée guy." The guy who orders the safe bet and keeps to his own little plate? Boring! Yawn! Next!

Food is life, and we're often territorial with things like food, fitness, friendships, relationships, and routines. All that stuff. Let go and come back to that valuable lesson you learned in kinder- garten to share your toys, and don't hog the red crayon! In my life, I tend to play it safe, I often get the chicken salad because it works and I like it. It's predictable, and I'm very rarely disappointed. But in exploring more variety, trying new things, and asking others to jump outside the box with you, you get to enjoy so much more!

There is something to be said for the impact you can make on me by just saying, "You wanna share appies?" It shows me that you are committed to exploring life together, being a part of a team, respecting and understanding diverse preferences, and that you are capable of enjoying and appreciating a variety of tastes and flavors. Teamwork is life. We are often alone, taking care of ourselves, ordering a safe meal because we know it will fill us up and do the trick. I love grabbing that menu for appies and that anticipation of all the ones I know and love, then my bestie saying,

"Hey, wanna add the salt and pepper chicken wings today too?"

"Sharing is caring!"

"Variety is the spice of life!"

Rescue your own damn self by surrounding yourself with people who will embrace some variety and share the damn appies, and live sassily ever after!

Sigh. Now I'm hungry for appies and thirsty for wine. Who is free to meet me at the Cactus Club?!

There Are No Regrets in Life, Just Lessons!

....

Shoulda, coulda, woulda!

Every decision.

Every step.

Every misstep.

Every fuck-up.

Every slipup.

Every mess-up.

Every good time.

Every challenging one.

They all lead us to where we are today.

They all form us into the person we are at this moment.

Everything has a purpose!

Everything that happens in our lives teaches us something.

In moments of upset or sadness, it's much harder to see that than when things are sailing smoothly.

It's easy to see perspective, feel joyful, and celebrate when there are moments of happiness throughout your life, or when everything is going according to the "plan." Whose plan is it anyway?!

Someone once told me, "The more times you fail, the more times you succeed." It hurts, though we often can't see it. In mistakes, we often struggle to find the lesson. It's with time and healing that it eventually comes to light if we let it.

Mistakes happen. But if you change the narrative and think of those mistakes as learning experiences that mold you for your next choices, it changes your perspective. Not dwelling can often push us toward the path we were supposed to be on. Often, that detour is what leads us on the greatest adventures.

We are always where we are supposed to be. We are always dealt the cards we are supposed to have. **And we are always thrown the curveballs that we can handle.** At the time, we were wondering what the hell the Universe was trying to teach us, but zoom out, take a step back, pause for a moment, and it usually becomes clear.

I have two children: Brooklyn, my oldest, and Beckham. But I was pregnant before I had Beckham. I remember the day I found out; I was so excited and told anyone who would listen. And I remember the tragic day, at thirteen weeks into the pregnancy, when I started spotting.

That was the end. I had a miscarriage.

I was devastated. My hormones were raging. I couldn't understand that kind of loss, when in reality, after talking to all of my friends and other women, it was much more common than any of us admitted to or discussed. My doctor told me to try again and brushed me off. I couldn't believe this happened to ME. I regretted getting pregnant. I was mad at myself because I was happy with one child, and living in this sadness was a lot to bear.

But I didn't give up tryin'! Soon after, I found out I was pregnant again and gave birth to an amazing baby boy. I realized that day that regret and sadness had taught me the lesson that everything happens for a reason. And that miscarriage enabled me to have Beckham, my son. He wouldn't be alive if that other pregnancy went to full term. His existence wouldn't BE. And that in itself was the lesson I learned.

Regrets are just ways in which we cope with things we don't like, don't understand, are uncomfortable with, angry about, and disgusted by. There are lots of reasons we might feel regret. Heck, eating a bag of cookies or consuming too much wine is something I see so often in my clients and friends. We sit in this pity party of emotions, dwelling, thinking we could or should change it. But it's in the past. Somehow it taught us a lesson, and we can move the frick forward! Learn, grow, know better next time, and do better next time.

Breakups are a huge wonderland of regret for us. If I had a dollar for every time I lost tears over some guy or had to console a friend who lost "the love of her life," I'd be rolling around on a bed of cash! Think about breakups. Afterward, we're bitter for the time we gave to that person. We replay conversations and moments, and we regret not handling it a different way. We regret the whole damn thing. Until we come out of the pain and eat our emotions away enough to see some light, then often that breakup helps us grow and find someone even better!

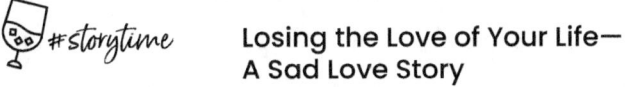 #storytime

Losing the Love of Your Life— A Sad Love Story

My client Lynn was in love. Hearts followed her everywhere she went. It was disgusting to see her and her husband, Tom, together because they needed to get a room. He gushed over her. He would constantly tell her how she was his soul mate, his life! Lynn quit her amazing high-powered corporate job in Toronto and moved her life to follow Tom to Vancouver for his "big break" in the film industry. When I first started coaching her, I would see them together and would just be in awe of their love. *How could I find this? Did it really exist?* Well, one day, Tom told Lynn he was in love with someone else and had been for years. He had actually moved them to Vancouver so he could be with this other woman. Lynn was devastated. He was her "everything." She regretted ever loving him, regretted leaving her career for a man who stomped on her heart and crushed her soul. It was a rough year for her. She was lost and full of regrets. What was life teaching her? In the moment, it was hard to not hate life, hate Tom, hate all of it. Regret was not allowing her to heal and feel. Then one day she met James in a local Starbucks. James was also new to town and fresh out of a messy breakup. I thought James was the real man of her dreams, but here's the true plot twist: she and James had an amazing love affair, then broke up. But he helped her love again. And he helped her forget the word "regret." James owned a massive corporation, and to this day Lynn is still COO of it. She has tons of money, an amazing downtown condo, and a great life! And she's married to someone who IS the love of her life. But if that asshole Tom and his fake love for Lynn hadn't made her uproot her whole life to Vancouver, she wouldn't have met James, wouldn't have healed her heart (an important part of finding love again is mending that broken heart!), and wouldn't have found a wonderful job, love, and life. She wouldn't have found herself so that in the end she could find someone she didn't have to uproot anything for. She was her best self from this whole traumatic experience.

Regrets are really just the mold for the experiences that shape us! #dropthemic

I'm not saying don't feel the pain, sadness, madness, and emotions. But in the moment when you are about to scream, "I regret this!" I want you to stop it! Change the storyline to "What is the lesson in this?"

Rescue your own damn self from getting on the regret train, and live sassily ever after!

I Want My Life as Sustainable as My Seafood!

....

The first time I heard the word "sustainability" or "sustainable," I was at a fancy restaurant in Lake Louise. I ordered the sea bass, and the server began to tell me that the fish was very hard to come by, and one we might not see in upcoming years because of its lack of "sustainability." I was intrigued. I had never thought of fish or wildlife as being endangered or wiped out. I never realized that the actions we had been taking, such as dwindling the supply, meant the future generations wouldn't be enjoying the buttery goodness of a good old sea bass covered in a cream sauce!

Who knew that life was about making choices in the present to avoid compromising our future?

 **#storytime** **The Application of Sustainability in Life— An Exploration**

Love—That whirlwind romance and hot sex is fun for short-term excitement. But having security and a solid foundation is what makes it a sustainable relationship that lasts a lifetime. The guy who is great in the sack but doesn't take out the garbage or bring you ginger ale when you're sick is for present day only. He's not the sustainable kinda love that will be there for you when you truly need him. The hot and heavy, coming on strong one-night stand with five orgasms isn't the same as the guy who picks you up when your car breaks down or stays up with you till 2 a.m. when you can't sleep because you're upset about something.

Fitness—The six times a week, beast-mode workouts seem like a great idea, until you overtrain, tire out, and can't keep up with the workload. The body gives out! Slow and steady wins the race. By starting small, you're more likely to sustain the scheduling and timing around it. Just as that crash diet with no calories was tolerable for the moment and yielded quick-fix results, the rebound when you binge eat and can't maintain it is a bitch! Any lost pounds come back quickly, and then some! Cutting out carbs seems like a good idea when your abs show up, but it's not sustainable when you just want a freakin' pizza!

Career—Working like a dog is great in your twenties when you take on overtime and juggle split shifts and long hours, until you burn out and can't keep up with the rigorous schedule. Hitting the ground running is great, until you hit a wall!

Making decisions in life is all about sustainability. Does it benefit you now *and* later? We do so much less damage to ourselves in the present when we have an eye on our future.

Just like we can wipe out an entire sea bass population from eating too much of it, we can wipe ourselves out and make our lives far harder to enjoy in the future.

Taking drugs and partying hard was fun in your twenties, but will you make it to eighty if you don't make a change now?

Not eating to nourish your body and living off boxed mac and cheese only works for so long. Till it doesn't. And your body shuts down from lack of proper nutrients.

Smoking. It's a vice now, but sustaining that results in a shorter life-span and so many other complications you don't realize you're signing up for with that first inhale.

That unprotected sex that ends with a child you didn't plan impacts what your life will look like later.

Rescue your own damn self by living like that endangered fish looking for sustainability, and live sassily ever after!

Aladdin

Finally, we see a flip in the script! It's now a princess and a random street rat trying to win her love! Finally, it's not about her quest for the handsome prince, although the princess's family was trying to set her up in an arranged marriage (which even in this day and age is still quite common in certain cultures).

Lori's *Fast and Furious* Fairy Tale Breakdown:

* Homeless street guy **Aladdin** meets Princess **Jasmine**, but he's just a guy with no job (like some of my exes!). And he's got a sneaky sidekick. (This movie made me want my own pet monkey!)
* **Jafar** (kinda like security or assistant to the king) sends Aladdin to find the magic lamp, which he does, and he meets **Genie**, a.k.a. Robin Williams (RIP. His Genie was SO much better than Will Smith's follow-up version. He should have stuck with *Men in Black*! Just sayin'!)

* Aladdin gets three wishes, which of course includes becoming someone he isn't so that the princess will fall for him and marry him. But he promises his bestie, the genie, that the last wish he will make will be to rescue him from that bottle and set him free. Another man making another promise he doesn't intend on keeping!

* Eventually, it all comes crumbling down: Jasmine realizes he's not a rich prince. Her papa sees their love and gets rid of the rule that she must marry a prince. And they wed and live happily ever after! Sidenote: Aladdin did end up keeping the promise to set the genie free! Legit, he picked freeing his friend over changing the laws to be able to have his fairy tale end happily. That's a good friend!

The Facade or Complete Insanity in a Nutshell:

* Man changes himself and pretends to be someone he isn't for a rich princess. Where to begin? This happens way more often than we'd like to admit. Ladies, get yourself a man who is real with you.

* We get three wishes and someone to grant them for us. Not a real thing! Trust me, I have done my share of rubbing! No wishes were granted!

Lori's Life Lessons Learned from this Fairy Tale
(I don't wanna rewrite it, I wanna learn from it!):

* Be yourself for goodness' sake. Let's stop pretending to be someone else to be loved. Be yourself, and the RIGHT one will come along and accept that!
* Friends first. #girlcode Yep, if I have one wish left, and it's between granting myself a million dollars or helping a friend, I'll pick the friend, hands down! If it's about granting myself perfect skin forever and that new Tesla or helping a friend be free of suffering, it's my bestie without hesitation. Friends first, always!

Okay, let's play a game. Close your eyes and think about what would happen if you stumbled upon that lamp. You rubbed it, and out came Robin Williams, a.k.a. Genie. Mine would always be Robin, or maybe Chris Farley—someone with humor, for sure! What are your three wishes? I love this game. Legit, do it. Write down your three. What were they?

My three wishes usually end up being something like:
1. Wine that never runs out!
2. Jason Momoa naked in my bedroom!
3. Eating anything I want without gaining weight!

I will dig deeper and try to share my bigger, more impactful ones. (Ones that don't involve booze, naked men, and resolving body image issues!)

Lori's three wishes:

1. Be happy.

2. Be healthy and feel good.

3. Ensure everyone I love is happy and feels good.

Okay, so those three things are shit I can actually grant myself! I don't need a random guy in a lamp! No rubbing or wishing needed! What if making these great things happen means you pull up your big girl panties and find a way to make that shit happen for yourself by stepping into your truth, your personal power? Owning your happiness and doing what it takes to find your joy. I can choose to be happy and make daily choices to ensure my own happiness. I can do things that keep my health in check and make sure all I do is so I can feel good. And the most important one, I can ensure the people around me are also happy and feeling good. So, my wishes are granted!

Rescue your own damn self by knowing you are your own genie in a lamp and can grant your own wishes and make your own dreams come true. Find your inner magic, and live sassily ever after!

Stop Giving a Shit About What Others Think!

....

Disclaimer: My first book, *Kiss My Curvy Assets*, and my podcast of the same name are both actually my way of telling people that "if they don't like what I say or do, kiss my ass!" I just put a nicer spin on it! But it's my motto to help me live sassily ever after. Giving fewer shits about what anyone else thinks.

"I wonder if this outfit makes everyone think I gained weight?"

"I'm so nervous to get up and speak at the board meeting. What are people saying or thinking about me?"

"That girl is looking at me strangely. I bet she's judging me."

Does this inner dialogue sound familiar? That was me for most of my life. Constantly worrying about what others were thinking about me. Their opinions, their judgments. My fear of gaining weight was always around what others might believe about me.

Why do the opinions of others (even random strangers) matter so much to us? Why do we live our lives and miss taking action on so many things for fear of how those around us will react? It's like we are walking on eggshells and treading ever so lightly for fear of the all-consuming opinions of people who don't matter in the grand scheme of things.

When was the last time you skipped doing something for fear of the thoughts of those around you? Once I finally said, "Fuck it," and did my thang, it just felt freeing. It just felt so much better to release the madness around me. Just do you, boo! Once I stopped giving a shit, I could finally stop the weight I would hold in terms of what everyone else thought of my actions. None yo' damn business!

"If you don't like how I dress, don't look!" became my new mantra!

If someone does choose to make negative comments about something you are doing or how you are looking, it says more about them than you! It's not you, it's them! Most of the time, it's their insecurities or their history spewing their fucked-up baseless opinions onto something as simple as what you are doing.

🍷 #storytime　**Dance, Dance, Dance**
(*Dirty Dancing*-style
#noonereplacesswayze)

My son is a wicked dancer. All the genres. But being a boy who dances is a stigma we are still trying to shake, even in our evolving society. At school, he would be teased for doing ballet. The other boys would bully him and tell him hockey or soccer was a "boy's" sport. Not ballet. They would call him gay and place their judgments. He didn't care, not one bit, because I taught him that he gets to do what he wants and loves, apart from whatever anyone else thinks. When they tell him boys aren't supposed to dance, he fires back, "Why not?" When they tell him ballet makes him gay, he tells them that his favorite color is pink and that doesn't mean he is gay. He also tells them they need to find another way to bully and put him down 'cause being gay isn't a bad thing either. Smart boy! Mama taught him well!

Back to the dancing. Mama loves to dance too! We both feel that dancing should be done anywhere and everywhere. In the grocery store when we hear the music in the background, we bust out a full montage or hip-hop dance numbers. We flipped the script on the old saying of "Dance like no one's watching." We think you should dance like everyone's watching and you don't care what they think. Or better yet, ask them to join in! So, in public, we dance. In line at the bank, we groove. In the car when a good song comes on, we crank it and sing at the top of our lungs. Usually, people smile at us at stoplights.

We once had an elderly gentleman join in on our dance routine. It was epic, like you see in musical numbers on Broadway. We were at a ballpark when my son was younger, and "Macarena" came on. Sorry, you are gonna be singing it for days; you're probably even groovin' to it right now. #sorrynotsorry When I heard the song, I immediately started doing the dance. I had about thirty people doing it with me by the end. It was fun, invigorating, and just empowering to dance my ass off. And life should be playful. If we can't have fun, why are we here?

How liberating will it be for you to just bust a move without the weight of others' judgment? What a load off to throw shit to the wind and just let out that crazy energy. People are going to judge you no matter what you do. Too fat, too thin, too loud, too reserved, too ____ (insert your too much). So, make the choices you want to make. Dye your hair purple and rock it at the office. Life is too short to not do what YOU want to do! BE who you want to be! Dance like a lunatic without worrying about what that mean *Dancing with the Stars* judge would say if they were watching you dance and picking your kick-ass dance routine apart.

Rescue your own damn self by not giving any shits about what anyone else thinks. And once you stop caring, live sassily ever after!

When Life Gives You Lemons, Make Vodka Lemonade!

....

When life gets hard, you take the punches . . . and get intoxicated! Just kidding!

But seriously, let's make the best of a difficult situation. I'll drink to that! Cheers!

Take a negative and make it a positive.

Embrace whatever comes your way!

Look on the bright side!

Be optimistic.

I was going to take this chapter and make it about starting your own business. Seeing the opportunity to take those lemons, get some venture capital, and open up the most kick-ass lemonade stand ever. But that's boring AF! Been there, done that!

I like to see the analogy of making vodka lemonade as how a goddess copes with or navigates the lemons, a.k.a. bullshit, that life throws her way. When life gets a little sour, how are you going to deal with those stressors?

We all have our vices. Being a mom is hard. Heck, being a woman is so fuckin' difficult sometimes! Here is a truth bomb: you have to suck it up and get through it! Life is going to toss a ton of shit at you, and just when you think it's done, it tosses even more. It's like a shit tornado, sometimes!

Character breakdown of copers:

The Avoider
Let's just pretend it didn't happen. Life got hard, and so you sidetrack yourself, push it down, stay busy, act like it's probably fine, and just keep putting one foot in front of the other.

The Emotional Outburst Queen
Difficult shit happens and you throw a massive temper tantrum like a kid crashing from a sugar high. Cry, scream, throw a fit of rage. That was how I managed things. But that got super draining, and it just wasn't the best method. I'd sob like a newborn baby and my eyes would be so swollen I could barely open them. Cry some more, scream more, then I would allow myself the release of emotions in a "healthier way." Like screaming into a pillow. Ya feel me?

The Zen Master
My therapist (bless her well-paid soul) once told me it might be better for me to take the stressful or emotional situation (sour lemons) and meditate or journal. For some, this is an amazing

way to cope with life's difficult stuff, but for me, this just made me angrier! More pent up and more frightened. Sit, meditate, breathe, reflect, and move forward . . . that's just not me. One of my fitness mentors, Barb, once went to a retreat in India for a few weeks. She would tell me stories where they would have to sit cross-legged and meditate in the scorching heat for sometimes up to three hours. When the trickle of sweat was sitting on the end of her nose, she wasn't to wipe it away or even move. She was to stay focused on her breathing. Ah, yeah, have you met me? I don't sit still for more than five minutes, let alone three hours of calm, quiet, and stillness. I remember once taking a meditation class at a local yoga studio. "Pitas, peanut butter, frozen fruit . . . check, check, check." My mind was going over my grocery list. "Life is hard, so hard, OMG, I'm so sad, I'm so upset, anxiety is climbing." Sitting still made my mind go to the tough situations and stress of life and magnify it, not rectify or calm it. So, if you're like me, find a different way to cope. Get moving, release the pent-up energy through a workout, dance, or having a scream party or punching some pillows. If this is you, yay! There are tons of meditation apps and free soundtracks and videos on YouTube that will help you Zen the eff out!

The Runaway Bride

This romantic comedy was epic. Maggie (Julia Roberts, always badass in the romantic genre) gets stressed out a bunch of times when she's about to get married and runs! This was me for a decade. Coping meant locking myself away in a tower and being the pouting princess. In high school, when I kept getting bullied, instead of facing those bullies, I would miss school for two whole weeks. Then when I assumed the bully had forgotten they wanted to beat me up or harass me, I could return. But running away works for only so long because your legs get tired, and you eventually have to deal with the situation. You eventually have to draw your sword, return to fight the greatest fight, and slay the dragons!

The Joker
Make light of things. Laugh about it. Add humor to make it seem not so difficult or negative. Joke and make it your bitch to deal with the insanity of certain things in life!

The Problem Solver / List Maker
My friend Anne is amazing at coping with the crap in life. She analyzes and maps out her strategies to cope. She understands, gathers information, and manages the problem like she manages her staff of twenty-five at her business. Control girl Anne to the rescue!

The Social Butterfly

Gather the girl squad and head on a wicked girls' weekend when life gets tough. That's a way to cope. Pass the vodka lemonade. Now, I am not promoting alcoholism, that would be bad of me, but I am promoting a release. Coping might look and feel like spending three days in Vegas where you drink too much, dance too much, eat too much, and just cope with life by hanging with your ladies and making terrible choices that fall under "what happens in Vegas, stays in Vegas!" #nojudgments I have so many stories to use as blackmail from stuff we've had go down on girls' trips, but my besties could equally bury me if they wanted to, so we stick by the gal-pal code that not even torture will make us tell. We can't always get away and jet off to amazing girl-power weekends, so this might be a trip to the local hot spot for dancing, drinking, and having fun. It might be setting up the stand in the front yard and your bestie brings the vodka and you provide the lemonade!

Out of all the coping characters above, you might find that you are a combination of a few. You mix and match the ways in which you deal with this "hard knock life." No one is better than the next, and I will never judge anyone for how they take life's punches and keep ensuring they can get themselves back up.

Rescue your own damn self by finding the way or ways that work for you. Lock yourself away in that tower if you need to, have the "ugly stepsister" temper tantrum and throw some shit, or set up shop in the front of your castle and pass the vodka lemonade, babe, and live sassily ever after!

Life Is Like the Self-Serve Checkout at Walmart!

Remember when you would go to a grocery or department store, and there would be line after line of eager cashiers ready to scan your groceries? Heck, this might shock you, but they used to also provide the plastic bags and actually bag your groceries for you! Gasp! Those who worked in the service industry (like me) actually provided *service* to the customers! Ah, the good old days!

Fast-forward and present day, you have to do everything for yourself. But is that really a bad life lesson or one we need to embrace?

In life, you need to be self-sufficient. Sure, we get help with some things, but we can't rely on it.

Just like every time I go to Walmart and see the one cashier who has twenty people in her line, and three other cashiers who are standing around doing nothing point me in the direction of the self-serve checkouts, I turn into my grandmother reminding my teens of the "olden days when I didn't have to do shit for myself!"

 **#storytime   Lori's Pumping Gas Adventures**

My name is Lori, and I didn't pump my own gas until I was

twenty-five-years old. In Ontario, where I'm from, you can get your driver's license when you're sixteen. I had already purchased an almost new fire-engine red Chrysler Daytona (OMG, I can't believe I considered it a hot sports car!). From the age of sixteen until twenty-five, I did not once pump my own gas. At first, it was for convenience or because my dad would fill up my tank for me without me having to ask. But that set me up for what would be almost a decade of a fear of pumping it myself. I was petrified. I would drive clear across the city or pass through small towns waiting to see a "Full Serve" sign. I would wait in line for an attendant to pump it for me, when the self-serve pumps were wide open. Because I'd never had to do it on my own, I didn't think I could. It was only when I had my daughter that I didn't have time to find that full-service station. She was crying and in need of her afternoon nap, so as I pulled up to the self-serve, I knew if I could handle a screaming baby, I could pump my own gas, damn it! I remember being scared, but I also remember feeling so proud after I did it. I pulled out of the station thinking, *I can take on the world!*

The same thing happened to the granny of a good friend of mine. She was still one of those people who went to the bank and stood in line for the teller to deposit her check. It's another "good old days" story when there were so many tellers happy to help you with your banking needs. Now, it's all about bank machines and no one to help you! Self-serve. You gotta take care of yourself. I get it; to an older person, it's daunting to deal with tech. For my friend's grandma, it was more of a trust issue of not knowing where that check went when you stuck it in the slot! But I remember the day she finally conquered that machine. I went with her and showed her how to deposit her check and withdraw some cash. Her expression when she was done was priceless. She was beaming with pride and almost strutted out of that bank because she did it herself. She "self-served!" Did it take her forever as she fumbled with codes and cards? Yep! But it also takes me a long time when I'm at the self-serve at Walmart. I hate it! You mean I'm the one "working" at Walmart today scanning and bagging my own items? Ugh!

Rescue your own damn self by knowing that life means you figure shit out yourself as you "self-serve," and live sassily ever after!

Four Weddings and a Funeral

Hugh Grant is in so many top romantic comedies. I'm kinda still waiting to find him attractive, like "leading man" attractive. Nope, not feeling it.

That being said, I am totally feeling this movie!

Timing is everything. Sometimes, love doesn't come together, YET!

Plot rundown:

- Charles (Grant) attends four weddings and a funeral (wow, that would make a great movie title!).

- He meets Carrie (Andie MacDowell), a beautiful American woman, at the first wedding, and it's love at first sight for both of them! (Not sure I believe that, but stay with the plot, as there's more to this story.)

- Insert hot sex and sleeping together like ten minutes after meeting (always!).

- Three more weddings happen, but something is always off and preventing them from coming back together. Heck, one of these weddings is even her wedding to another man! There's also a funeral, where they meet again. The fourth wedding is Charles's, also proving that the Universe has spoken, and it must not be "meant to be."

- But wait. Just when he was about to say "I do" to someone else, he says, "I don't. Carrie is my one true love." She obviously says, "I do too" . . . and they FINALLY live happily ever after together!

Okay, whew! I'm exhausted.

I like to think I'm a hopeless romantic who believes that if it's meant to be, it will be. That you will, when the timing is right, be with your soul mate, that one true love, no matter the odds.

Back up, though! You are a cynic now, and that belief is from watching too many romantic comedies, Lori!

Timing is everything! But missed opportunities often stack the cards against us. Heartbreak and constantly eroding trust makes an "unbreakable bond" breakable!

Let's look at the concept of timing, and why I think it's a game changer in love!

Say you meet someone and your heart skips a beat. But you are both in happy relationships (or what you think are happy). So, you part ways without the chance to make it work. Ten years later, when you run into one another at a party, you are both now single. Hmm, timing is everything. Maybe it's time to finally give it a shot.

I also like the concept of growing up. I know when I was eighteen, twenty, and even twenty-five, I didn't have the knowledge of what I needed or wanted. Now, at forty-five, you better believe I'm able to ask for what I want. I almost demand it. So, meeting someone much later again in life probably means I'm going to pull out all the stops and it might work out!

Location can often be another "timing is everything" moment. You meet someone on vacation, but they live in another city far away from you, so you don't have a long-distance love affair. Then ten years later you enter a Starbucks and there sits George, the hot guy from the pool you met a decade ago who stole your heart. He now lives in your city.

But to play devil's advocate here, I want to say I believe that if it was really meant to be, it would have been, despite the circumstances. I try to hold out the hope that ten years later, it would just come back and be some undeniable true love. Or what could have been is now something that doesn't make my older, wiser heart skip any beats! I'm more skeptical. Years have passed, and he didn't move mountains or cities for me back then, so why should I stop and look his way at Starbucks now? (Yep, still holding out for that Starbucks sponsorship!)

I get it; we want that happily ever after because of the damn rom-coms! But the practical gal in me has a more realistic plot twist.

Four Weddings and a Funeral—Lori's version:

- They meet, they have sex. (edit: HOT sex!)
- They meet again and again, then again (at her wedding).
- They meet again at a funeral. (Gotta keep with that title!)
- Finally, they meet again at his wedding, and he doesn't marry the poor lady at the altar he has been stringing along and doesn't love anyway. He soul searches and doesn't end up with Carrie, after all. He has some growing up and inner work to do. He needs to take a year to himself to find out why he's been playing mind games with everyone.
- Eventually, years later, he meets a nice girl, falls in love, and finally settles down. And Carrie meets someone else too. They're happy with other people and NOT together in the end.

Mine wouldn't be a box office hit, but hey, it's reality. **Don't sit back and let timing be everything. If it feels like it's right, make that shit happen now. Tomorrow might never come, so shit or get off the fuckin' pot!**

Rescue your own damn self by believing that timing is everything, knowing that even with timing or circumstance, sometimes it doesn't work out, and live sassily ever after!

Recharge the Battery, Fill the Gas Tank, Refill Your Cup!

....

Self-care is a trend we see talked about a lot in the media and online.

But what the heck does it even mean?

Taking care of yourself. Sure, that sounds like a piece of cake. But do we do it?

I saw an image online of a woman lying sideways with an empty battery slot in her back and a battery on the ground beside her. THAT is someone who didn't focus on self-care!

How many times have you known your battery was about to die, yet you kept on pushing?

Like how I was always the Energizer Bunny, we assume that we can just keep "going and going," but one day we're going to run out of juice and stop. This is a great analogy for life. We push, we hustle, we hit it, we bust our balls, we go, go, go. Till we just can't anymore.

It reminds me of what my father taught me growing up. He was a stickler for always filling the gas tank. Obsessed might be an understatement. He never wanted the gas tank to go much below half a tank, and never ever below a quarter of a tank. I was one of the ride-or-die girls. I liked seeing how low I could get the tank, how long I could drive with that flashing "E" begging me to pull into a gas station. The car would be completely empty and running on fumes as I finally decided to fill 'er up. He would lose it on me every time he checked my car. "Lori, there are gas stations everywhere. It takes two minutes to stop and refill your tank."

His reasoning is one I now accept in life. You see, when you get to the bottom of the tank, you're burning old gas. The shit that's leftover, and it's going to hurt your engine. Your car won't be running as smoothly. It'll be sluggish. Or worse, you will run out of gas and be stuck in the middle of nowhere!

In life, when we ignore the signs of almost being out of gas, we're using the bottom of the barrel of ourselves as well. We aren't as focused. We're more scattered or sluggish. Soon, we don't have anything in the tank to give.

He used to use the Ferrari analogy too. You wouldn't buy this super expensive sports car, then not change the oil or refill it with premium gas. And you surely wouldn't let it run on fumes and damage that costly engine. (Oh, how I regret all the massive eye rolls I gave him as a teen; this was deep shit he was teaching me!)

Why aren't we treating ourselves like a Ferrari? Why aren't we ensuring we have the best care and best fuel possible?

As moms, we do it all. We take care of our kids (meals to make, schedules to manage, rides to give), we take care of the house (cooking and cleaning), we have work to do and bills to pay, and we juggle to get it all done. But if we drop one of those balls, we're in trouble. And what if the ball that gets dropped is you? Your self-care. When you drop the ball on *yourself,* there's no one left to juggle for you. The kids who need rides are stranded or have to call an Uber or even worse, take public transit—the horror!

There is a reason on planes we are told to put our mask on first, then the mask of anyone else who needs help. If we go down, we can't help anyone else, so self-care is vital. Without it, we're gasping for air and passing out, which isn't good for anyone.

For me, self-care can be a day of shutting off social media or the world and binge-watching lame-ass comedies on Netflix.

For me, self-care can be a meal out with the girls, so we can all bitch about having to wipe piss off the toilet seats from our disgusting teenage sons! #whenyaknowyaknow

For me, self-care can be walking the dog to clear my mind and taking a break from everything for a while.

Without self-care, the body will eventually run out of gas.

Our mental and physical health will eventually need a battery recharge.

We need to refill our cup and reset. Overfill your cup if you need to so you have ample energy to keep you revved up when ya need it!

Rescue your own damn self by keeping that elite sports car of yours filled with premium fuel, and live sassily ever after!

Don't Let the Teeter-Totter Break Your Vagina!

Va-jay-jays everywhere are cringing at the thought of the seesaw or teeter-totter. Y'all know what I'm talking about—that piece of playground equipment that seemed fun at the time (up, down, up, down, good times) until WHAM! Vagina damage as we plummeted to the ground and tried to avoid long-term injury and the potential inability to have children.

Disclaimer: This park nightmare has been replaced in recent years. I have kids now, and upon venturing out to numerous playgrounds with them, I realized there must have been enough lawsuits to ensure the city needed to replace them with new springy versions that avoid vagina smashing!

Okay, back to this life lesson. You would think I was going to talk about trust issues, and boy, do I have a lot of PTSD because of this insane contraption. Like not trusting your stupid brother who has your feet dangling, holding you in the air 'cause he weighed more than you, and saying he would only let you down if you said he was smarter, and if you promised him your dessert at dinner. And just as the trust was there, he would push up with all his might and plummet your ass so hard to the ground. WHAM!

But this one is all about balance! And finding your sweet spot!

You see, for the teeter-totter to work (without any internal damage to either rider), you need to have almost equally weighted people on either side. You couldn't have your one-hundred-fifty-pound brother, if you were only one hundred pounds. So, it was usually me and my friend Cassie, because we both weighed the same. If Cassie jumped off midway (it happened, you know it did, damn it, Cassie!), the balance was affected.

Life is about balance.

Even weight.

Equal distribution.

Same proportions.

Keep it steady and in control.

Balance can also be about having many things in your life that operate on equal ground.

 #storytime **Work/Life Balance—
A Tightrope Adventure**

"I'm just trying to keep a great work/life balance," I say on a daily basis.

Juggling the online coaching business that has my phone lighting up with text messages, annoying calls, and endless Instagram DMs of clients leaning on me for support and guidance and needing questions answered is A LOT! Like 24/7, 365. So, when I realize things are out of balance, I put my phone away.

We all need to have boundaries. And we need to realize that work questions that come in on a Sunday can usually wait until Monday for an answer. I'm not a surgeon, after all. This isn't life or death!

Because we're slaves to our phones, it's hard in a lot of industries to shut off the work and find time to play. But if our work/life balance is too lopsided and we're living to work, life says F-U!

I use the teeter-totter to remind me of balance often, but my friend Brad sees it much differently. He thinks of the game Twister. In that game, balance isn't meant to keep an even kilter, it's about not falling on your ass. (I suck at Twister, by the way, so don't ask me to play. My attention span and competitive nature won't allow it!) In his analogy, Twister is more of a team sport, where other people can help you keep your balance. To not fall over, you need to lean on them. Childcare is a good example of this. We're parents and we need to work, but someone needs to watch over our kids so we can make the bucks to pay the bills! Insert a babysitter or nanny or childcare provider. Their help allows us to get our job done while ensuring the kids are supervised and kept alive.

Carpooling is another way of keeping the balance. We want to save the environment by lowering emissions, but we can't do it alone and need to rely on someone else to help us keep the balance of that by sharing drive time and saving gas.

Balance in how we eat and nourish ourselves is another way we create that centered seesaw. A green veggie here *and* a cookie there. Drink water most of the time *and* enjoy a glass or two of Pinot Grigio. In that comparison, balance doesn't have to be totally equal. I mean, we aren't drinking the same amount of wine as water. (Hey, stop pointing fingers! I am pretty sure I drink more water!) Balance can look and feel like 80/20, 70/30, 60/40, or 50/50. The key is in finding the balance scenario that works for you, while ensuring you don't damage your liver and can still function on a daily basis!

Rescue your own damn self, and don't let the teeter-totter break your va-jay-jay, girl. Stay balanced, and live sassily ever after!

U Can't Make Sense of Insensibility!

....

"You can't reason with crazy!" This was something a dear friend of mine would remind me of when I would be trying to make sense of a situation or the action of someone else.

"Lori, you can question, dissect, try to reason with, or explain it, but in the end, it's like knocking on a door with no one home. They aren't gonna answer!"

You will drive yourself mental trying to reason with something that is unexplainable. Trying to have conversations with someone who is not accepting of your differing views will drive you bonkers.

In the fitness industry, I often spend most of my time trying to reason with crazy methods, insane programming, and just complete nonsense. As I try to explain the crazy out of it, I tire myself out. It's comical to think back to the amount of wasted time spent trying to reason with the insanity!

Trying to explain the unexplainable is another way we will never find resolution. It's like being on a treadmill going nowhere. Like sitting in an elevator and pushing all the buttons, but it doesn't budge 'cause it's out of order.

I once worked with a woman who, no matter what you did

or said, would spin it into some attack on her. It would totally baffle me. *Did I say something wrong? Did I not handle that situation properly?* I used to stay up at night losing my precious beauty sleep trying to break it down to figure out what the heck was wrong with ME. Then one day, another staff member pointed out that it wasn't me who was causing these issues, it was her! This was something she did no matter what the situation was or how it was handled. She would always cause drama and make something major out of something minor. Trying to explain it or trying to change my actions to "fix" things always resulted in the same outcome. And I didn't understand because "you can't reason with crazy!"

Arguing on social media is another time I often see new levels of crazy people come out of the woodwork! You have a valid point, and someone has a differing point. You try to explain your side, but they won't listen at all. Legit points. Heck, sometimes you're clearly in the right, but nope, you are WRONG in their eyes. They almost skim past anything you have to say. Save the trouble of explaining yourself. You don't need to expend that precious energy.

Bullies, manipulators, liars, or abusers are all people who you cannot reason with. Crazy!

I was in a "relationship" in my late teens (I use that term *relationship* loosely since it was very one-sided: my side putting in all the effort, the other side doing all the using!). Years after we stopped speaking, I would try to explain why I was treated that way. *Something had to be wrong with me, right? If only I had done this or that.* For decades I would drive myself mad and continue to replay fights, moments I was belittled by them, the sadness, and heartbreak. I harbored emotional baggage from thinking I was not worthy or less than. Then I had my aha moment of *OMG! This is a "you can't reason with crazy" moment!* The unexplained was something I never would have been able to make sense of! As soon as I accepted this, it was like I was released from this prison I let myself be locked up in.

People will only hold as much power over you and your responses as you give to them. Regulate your nervous system, master your emotions by looking at facts as well as feelings, and quit trying to rationalize toxic behavior or patterns.

Rescue your own damn self by identifying and leaving those situations that are batshit crazy or involve toxic people without trying to make sense of them, and live sassily ever after!

The Wedding Singer

I will NEVER pick apart anything Adam Sandler and Drew Barrymore star in together. These two are the epitome of romantic comedy couples! I buy it, I believe it, and I won't second-guess it!

The Wedding Singer plot:

- Broke wedding singer Robbie (Sandler) gets stood up at the altar by his high school love because she thinks he's a loser who's going nowhere!
- He meets Julia, a waitress (Barrymore), and falls for her.
- She falls for him, but she's engaged to a super-rich hunk, who is a complete jerk.
- Finally, in the end, the wedding singer wins the girl over by of course singing her a song about growing old with her, which gets me every time! I mean, who wouldn't want the guy with Van Halen T-shirts you can wear as pajamas? And they lived happily ever after.

Now some takeaways before I make some observations or conclusions:

- It's okay to be unlucky in love, heartbroken, at your low point, and left at the altar. Let it be! You'll find someone new!

- If all else fails, sing a song to get the girl. It works every time!

- Your career or bank account doesn't define you. Love comes to us in so many forms, beyond looks, income, or status.

- Ninety-year-old ladies are super cute as rappers (you have to see the movie to understand). "Rapper's Delight" never sounded so great! This movie has the best soundtrack ever!

I also want to point this out: Sometimes, the one you choose and say yes to ends up not being *the one*. They are NOT your fairy tale. Sometimes, when you truly listen to your gut, you just know it's time to call it off 'cause they're not "meant for you."

I had a good friend once who called off her wedding one week before the big day. So much money was lost, and it was one of the toughest decisions I watched someone make. She came from this big Italian family, too, and her parents were so scary. But when she told them she realized it wasn't what she wanted, they were supportive and told her, "We want you to be happy and do what is best for you!"

Another friend has been engaged three times but has never

married because she realized (thankfully before spending a shitload of money) that it wasn't the final chapter of her fairy tale after all.

We can change our minds! We can pivot; we can detour.

We can run into someone new at Starbucks (#namedropagain) and realize our needs and dreams aren't all being met currently, and that it's okay to make a new game plan!

Make the hard decisions, and don't fear judgment. This is the one life we get, and if that means losing $10,000 on a wedding dress because you realize you're not ready, then make the call. Your happiness matters. Your desires matter. YOU matter. You can't please everyone, nor are you here to bite your tongue and censor your truth. So, have the tough conversations, make the hard decisions, and save yourself a lifetime of heartache and trouble, especially if you know deep within that you are not in a relationship that feels right for you.

So, in this movie, I really do want them to live happily ever after. I don't want them to worry about money or a career. I want LOVE to win this one time!

Rescue your own damn self by believing that love is not attached to dolla' bills or bank account balances, and that in the end, love can change. You can decide to make the difficult choices, and live sassily ever after!

Haters Gonna Hate, You Can't Be Everything to Everyone!

....

You only have to like yourself. Period.

Easier said than done to a self-proclaimed people-pleasing "has to be liked by everyone" gal like me!

My name is Lori, and my whole life I have always given too many shits about what others think of me. I spent my youth walking on eggshells, praying I didn't go against the grain, or ruffle any feathers. I spent my teens petrified that someone wouldn't like me. I made so many choices that I didn't want, choices that to this day I look back on with sadness and regret.

#truthbomb: There is always gonna be someone who doesn't like you. The planet is massive. Huge! Tons of personalities and people who have a different mindset or mentality. People who aren't happy with themselves, so they project it onto those around them.

A girl in high school once told me that she didn't "like my face." Legit, that was her reason. She actually said, "I hate your face." I remember being bullied by her. God, I was petrified of her, and I would be on pins and needles if she was at the same party as me. She was a bitch with a capital B! She made me sob myself silly. I would skip school just to avoid her when she was in her little rages of "hating on Lori." This continued for four years of high school. It was weird, too, because we had been good friends in junior high.

I lost sleep trying to figure out what I could have done to upset her. I tried harder and harder to "win her over." It wasn't until grade twelve that I finally had the balls to say enough! I cornered her and asked, "What the fuck is your problem? And why do you hate me?"

Her response is one I take with me in life when anyone doesn't like me. "Huh, I don't even remember why I hate you, Lori!"

That was her response. You see, she didn't lose any sleep hating me. She didn't care about the tears she was making me shed. Her hating me said more about her than me all along! When I played into her hatred, since she didn't even have a real reason, it made me weaker to her, like an easy target, and she fed into this and kept the "fake hate" going.

In adult relationships, this same song and dance happens too. Often, some random dude doesn't like a girl, and she spends years sobbing about it, trying to justify it, question it, and goes to therapy to unravel what's "wrong" with her. What if it was just that you weren't the girl for him? We can't be everything to everyone. What if you had blonde hair and he liked brunettes?

What if the way you chewed your food just turned him off? What if, and this happens a lot, he just met someone else who checked more boxes in terms of what he was looking for? What if he wasn't secure in himself and pushed you away because he didn't want to be found out?

It's easy to tell someone, "Don't care what others think, just do you, boo!" or "Not everyone is gonna like you and that's okay." *But easier said than done, Lori!*

One thing I learned in this life lesson is that if we allow others to have that power over us (really, you liking yourself is all that matters), it's like they have the ability to capture you, lock you in that tower, and throw away the key. It's like they've taken you hostage!

There is always someone who will think you are ugly. Who cares! There are equally if not more who see you as beautiful. And most importantly, you need to see yourself and your hotness!

There is always someone who will think you are stupid or not as smart as them. Who cares?! I realized there are a ton of people in the world with different smarts. You might be more book smart than me, but I can trump you on a variety of topics, hands down! If I am solid in my own self-worth, no one can make me feel less than just because my IQ is lower than theirs.

There is always someone who will think you are a "loser" or have a lower social status than them. So, don't run in my circle then, bitch! I did this in high school when I tried to fit in with every single crowd. How can you get the popular kids to like you and also protect the "geeks" from being bullied by them and also roll with the skaters and alternative kids while wearing your sports uniform 'cause you're also trying to mesh with all the athletes? **You can't be everything to everyone! It's exhausting and impossible.** But what you can be is unique to yourself. Your own person. Be who and what you want! And fuck 'em if that isn't their cup of tea! Some of us drink coffee! Some of us don't drink hot beverages and instead consume an excess amount of Pinot Grigio on ice (it's me, I'm someone!).

Rescue your own damn self from endless people pleasing or thinking that everyone needs to accept your greatness, and live sassily ever after!

Can't Keep a Houseplant or Goldfish Alive? Get a Kid Instead!

....

Parents, where ya at? Mamas, you're gonna feel me on this one!

June 1, 2002, I became a parent for the first time.

For over nine months, I read and reread *What to Expect When You're Expecting*. Google wasn't as mainstream back then, so we bought books from the local bookstore in person, not online through Amazon. The struggle was real. I got books on nursing, sleep training, parenting, and burping like a badass. (Well, that last one isn't a real book, but it should be! Other useful titles would be *How to Wipe Asses More Than You Ever Think You Will*; *Emotionally Drain Yourself to Feed Those Ungrateful Souls*; and *Physical Milestones for Babies That Yours Will Never Live Up To, So You'll Feel Like a Failure*!) I was obsessed. I was ready. I was prepped and saying, "Bring it on!"

I gave birth on the first of June, after two days of insane back labor, a birth plan that went right out the window, drugs when I said I was gonna be "fine without the drugs," and an extremely messed up episiotomy (when ya know, ya know—let's take a pause here to remember the perfect vaginas everywhere and thank them for their service! A moment of silence for all the messed up va-jay-jays from labor and delivery!). And mere minutes later, as I looked down at this little sleeping baby and I couldn't formulate a sentence from utter exhaustion, they sent me on my way with the car seat carrier in tow.

What. In. The. Actual. Fuck! was my first thought as I set the carrier down on the glowing hardwood in my posh downtown condo.

Who in their right mind let me leave the hospital with a baby?!

We aren't gonna make it forty-eight hours without some tragic loss. Take her back. I can't do this!

Show of hands. Who was like me and thought you wanted this, you worked for this, you studied hard for this, and the "Mom of the Year Award" goes to . . . NOT ME!

Burn the books, forget anything you read, heard, googled, watched a Netflix special on, or had your grandma tell you. You ain't gonna need it!

That little bundle of crying madness is now in charge of what's gonna happen, friends!

Control? WTF is that! You have no control. They do!

Power? Yeah, also let go of that.

Do this, not that, that's another urban legend that YOU think YOU actually get to decide. Wrong!

Throw shit to the wind and understand that no matter how much planning you did, it's a crapshoot now! From now on, *adaptability* will be your game plan. Only the strong will survive!

That's not a life lesson to scare the shit out of any parents-to-be, it's a fact I am happy to share. The lesson is that no matter how much you fuck things up, how many times your baby sits in a dirty diaper and you didn't even know, how many moments they just won't take the damn nipple, you're going to be just fine! And so are they! No matter how many dinners become temper tantrums and result in eating chocolate (for both you and the kid!). Or how many times at the end of a tragedy-filled meltdown of a day, you put them to bed and think, "Yep, made it through another one!"

 **#storytime**   **Rest in Peace, DeAndre!**

My name is Lori, and I cannot keep a houseplant alive to save my own life. I go and buy it. I water it. I talk to it constantly. I put it near the amount of sunlight I am supposed to. Then . . . WHAM! Brown and dead! Every single time!

My name is Lori, and I cannot be trusted with goldfish. My daughter worked at a local pet store and got a goldfish when she was fifteen. "DeAndre" was his name. I haven't altered it for I feel I need to pay tribute to dear old DeAndre and the crime I committed. This fish lived through a fifteen-year-old taking care of it! She kept him in her cold, dark, dirty, and disgusting teenage girl bedroom. She rarely fed him. He was quite neglected, to say the least. But he was gold and flourishing! When my kids left to visit their grandparents at the lake that summer, I was left in charge of DeAndre. I mean I had a dog I kept alive, so a fish should have been no problem. Well, I decided to move him to the kitchen where I wouldn't forget to feed him. Like clockwork, I fed him fish food daily. I even talked to him. Then one day I was feeding him and noticed he seemed to be enjoying a longer than usual nap. *He's fine, I'm sure. Just sleeping. Probably exhausted.* Hmm, I searched online: "What does it mean when a fish is *sleeping* with its eyes bulging open?" I was still in denial. As I stuck my hand into the bowl to "startle" him awake, I noticed mold growing on him. Then I realized: *I killed DeAndre!*

Leave your kids with me, your puppies and dogs, too, but never ever think your plant or fish will be okay in my care.

Back to keeping kids alive. I have a nineteen-year-old and a fifteen-year-old. One made it to adulthood; the second one, although he sleeps away most of the twenty-four hours of his daily existence, should see the light of day ahead!

How the heck is that possible?

I didn't follow the "rules" I was supposed to.

Little secret: There are no rules and there are no right ways to do things. And no one else knows what the heck they are doing either. It's all a gamble. You toss the dice and hope for the best!

Breast is best was for sure invented by a man who never had a screaming, tired, hungry baby, who didn't know how to latch or have the patience to learn. And that "rule" didn't help a nervous mama who was having a meltdown and was at her wits' end and really trying her best!

"Breastfeeding is the most natural and amazing connection on the planet," says the person who hasn't suffered mastitis (an engorgement of the ducts causing insane fevers, delusional outbreaks, and boobs the size of Japan that are so tender to the touch I am tearing up right now thinking about it!). They haven't been sitting up exhausted at 3 a.m. with cold nipples so raw that just the thought of your baby trying to latch makes your toes curl (I'm surely not gonna be sponsored by La Leche League!).

"But the book says . . ." is the stupidest sentence I have ever uttered in my mere existence. And I said this a lot during the first six months of my daughter's life. "The book says if I try the football position, her *little princess lips* will latch better." The book was wrong!

The book didn't tell me that when I had mastitis, my tits would be so sore I would almost vomit. The book forgot to mention that I would go to the local drop-in medical clinic looking like a screwed-up version of my disgusting mess of myself and the doctor on call would be thirty and a Jude Law look-alike with the body of Mark Wahlberg saying to me, "So, let's take a look at this engorged breast!" #killmenow

Eventually, I was lucky enough to push through the agony of the "natural disaster" called breastfeeding, and both kids were breastfed for almost too long IMO! But many of my friends were not as lucky. Or was it not about "luck" at all? Sometimes, depending on certain factors, breastfeeding wasn't even an option. That's just how it would be, and that's okay.

My baby group mom friend Jessica had the cutest little guy Evan. She tried so hard to breastfeed. She would show up to the mom meetings sobbing because he wouldn't eat and he cried all day. "But the book says . . ."

One day Jessica went to her doctor's office, and he took her by both shoulders and said, "Your son is starving to death. I get that this book told you breast is best, hell, my colleagues in medicine keep promoting it as the be-all and end-all. But Mama, he is dying of starvation. Give him the fuckin' formula; it's not poison!" Within moments of him sucking on that bottle and getting the formula, Evan was happy and healthy, and Jessica tried to never look back. Still, she felt like a "failure" because it wasn't what the book said. Stop the madness! The book is wrong. Do what works for you and what keeps your "houseplant" alive! Don't feel like a failure just 'cause the book tells you that you didn't follow their "rules." There are no rules, remember?!

Your baby is in control of how it's gonna be! Fed is best, no matter what that looks like.

Formula exists for a reason, and so does your gut instinct. So when the book says to just cry it out, don't cry it out like me in the corner, 'cause when I tried that it didn't work for me and my two babies. Even though the book said . . . Shut up, book!

When you have toddlers and they will only eat grilled cheese and Goldfish crackers for a whole year straight and nothing else, the book says they won't get the nourishment they need, but here's a little secret—they will be okay!

When your eight-year-old goes through a phase of only wanting "waffles" for dinner, it's okay! They will eventually tire of the waffles and want a damn vegetable!

I didn't feed my kids cow's milk. They went from breast to nothing. I didn't "fortify" anything, I didn't rice milk it, I didn't overthink it. Didn't tabulate the amount of calcium needed in broccoli to make up for the missing vitamins. I just fed them. And they are built like brick shit houses now! Their bones are just fine.

Those moments when other mothers are judging you, please look back at them and think, *Your shit stinks too, sista.* Don't let them pass the *mom judgments.* In fact, we all need to stop judging one another.

When you are so tired you think you will never sleep again, you will! I promise.

When you think you've fucked up your kids so much and are going to parent prison because you are unsure if you're doing it "how the book says," forget about it! They can get a therapist like the rest of us when they are older!

Unlike those houseplants or goldfish, the kids are gonna make it! They're gonna be all right. If I have not just one, but two kids who I didn't screw up too badly, anyone can do it!

Rescue your own damn self by knowing you are trying your best because parenting is freakin' hard. At the end of the day, your kids will eventually become adults, who will then call YOU when they have a newborn at home saying, "But, Mom, the book says . . ." and live sassily ever after!

Someone Always Has It Worse Than You!

In times of despair or when things are just plain shitty, I always remind myself that it could be worse. Now, this isn't to be confused with bottling up my feelings or not letting myself have a full-blown Lori "ugly cry it out" few minutes, hours, or even a Netflix sobfest for days, if needed.

Be sad, be angry, and hate the moments that are freakin' hard. But when life throws curveballs, tragedies, losses, or WTF moments, holding on to the thought that *someone out there has it worse than me* enables us all to push forward and get through it!

#storytime Eye-Opening Moments

I had a client, Dianne, who once volunteered to sleep outside for homeless youth. It was an event put on by the Vancouver chapter of Covenant House, an organization that helps teens who are living on the streets, something I wish would never happen to anyone as a teen, or heck, even an adult. For one night, volunteers show up to the downtown location to sleep on the street overnight. It was dark and cold, and since it's Vancouver, it was wet and raining too. She asked me to do it with her, but I had to decline since I hate being cold and knew I would be sobbing hysterically or running for the hills an hour in! Remember, this is just one night, not the weeks, months, or even years, that most of the homeless population endure. Dianne had an expensive sleeping bag, lots of warm clothing, and a full belly as she went into her one night of "homelessness." She even drove to this "sleep out" in her BMW with heated seats!

At our session together a few days later, I remember her telling me this story as her eyes filled with tears. "Lori, we are so lucky. Our kids are so lucky. We don't realize how terrible it is to be on the streets, with no warm bed or safe space to sleep."

She said she got to meet a lot of homeless teens and to hear their stories. Their fears and their struggles would shock you. One teen shared how she had been on the streets for almost a year, always hungry and always cold. Most frightening of all was that she lived in fear of being attacked by some of the mentally unstable or druggies in the neighborhood. She was afraid of being robbed in her sleep and losing what little she did have. "But there's always someone out there who has it worse than me!" the teen said.

This doesn't have to just be homelessness. During the pandemic, we saw so many around us lose their jobs or lose a loved one. Seeing someone worse off can definitely snap us into appreciating the life we do have.

I've had so many friends who have suffered miscarriages or

have lost children who use this principle to find gratitude again. They are thankful that they were able to get pregnant in the first place, as many women and couples aren't so blessed. They've found the silver lining in the sadness and loss.

My mother battled with breast cancer when I was in my late teens and beat it, thankfully. But I remember when she first got her diagnosis, she went through a period of despair, questioning "why me?" When she started treatment at the cancer clinic, she saw two little bald children giggling away and coloring while receiving their treatments. That's when it hit her that there was someone who had it worse. She exclaimed to me, "I have grown children, and I've led a long life. If those two very young kids can keep a positive, happy attitude through something they should never have to battle, then I need to smarten the heck up and also fight the fight!" It was at that moment she adopted the same "someone has it worse" analogy.

Whether it's a hardship or a heartbreak, it's tough during times of any amount of suffering to be thankful for what we still do have. Taking a moment to understand and witness the difficulties that others face can jolt us back into deeper appreciation and intentionality with our own life. It helps us to move ahead and deal with life's shittiest times or darkest moments.

Rescue your own damn self by knowing that even the person out there who truly does have it the complete worst, still has hope and a willingness to persevere. Life is hella messy. But get gritty, get bold, and live sassily ever after!

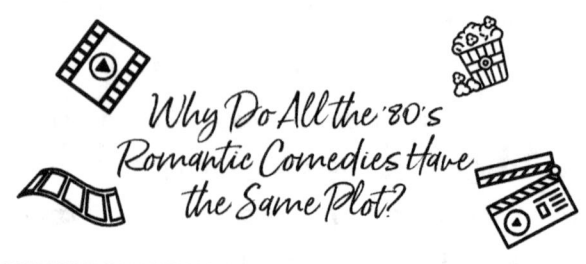

Why Do All the '80's Romantic Comedies Have the Same Plot?

- Guy meets girl. Guy's family is rich. The girl's family is poor.

OR

- Girl meets guy, she's from a wealthy family, and he's from the trailer park.

OR

- Guy meets girl, but she's a dork, and he's popular.

Ever notice that every single '80's romantic comedy has the same plot?

Sixteen Candles—Girl is a geek; guy is a popular jock. Against the odds, hunky Jake (Michael Schoeffling) picks dorky Samantha (Molly Ringwald). You know the moment. He's outside the church at her sister's wedding, leaned up against his red sports car (in a sweater vest, a major fashion failure). He waves to her. She turns around to look behind her and mouths: "Who me?" He nods and mouths back: "Yeah, you!" Insert my heart throbbing! This is love, people!

Pretty in Pink—This is the exact same plot as *Sixteen Candles*! It even stars Molly Ringwald again, although in this film, she's from a broken family and is poor. The boy (Andrew McCarthy) is from a wealthy family. They fall in love, but it's hard for them to be together without getting judged by their circles for dating outside their groups. Still, they say, "Hey, I want to do this!" And they end up together happily ever after! Sidenote: I always thought she should have picked her best friend (Duckie), who was madly in love with her and also from the same side of the tracks.

The Breakfast Club—Welcome back again, Molly Ringwald! What's that? You were expecting a plot twist? I wish! Again, same plot, only this time, it's multiple kids in detention. Multiple opposites attracting. Good girl Claire (Ringwald) and bad boy John (Judd Nelson); preppy jock (Emilio Estevez) and goth girl (Ally Sheedy). Everyone meets, but they think it could never work out because they are in detention, and once they leave, reality will tear them apart, you know, because of the social hierarchy of high school. In the final scene, John pumps his fist in the air (like power to the people that we can and will break free and all be together) while Simple Minds sings "Don't You (Forget About Me)." Hey wait? Does that song mean they don't actually get to be together because of society's restrictions and beliefs? Who knew?!

Say Anything—Finally an '80's movie without Molly Ringwald! Boy (John Cusack) and girl (Ione Skye) from different lives (shocker) fall in love. The only reason I even post about this movie is *that* scene. You know the one. It tugs at our hearts and confirms that soul mates exist. Boy stands outside of his crush's window, holding a boom box up in the air on full blast (for the youngsters, a boom box is the '80's version of what we now call a Bluetooth speaker!) playing Peter Gabriel's "In Your Eyes." The way to my heart in all honesty is to stand outside my window with a speaker blaring this song, and I'm yours for life! (And if you also bring a chilled bottle of Pinot Grigio—wow!) I think this movie has ruined me for all romantic gestures!

Roxanne—In an updated version of *Cyrano de Bergerac*, boy (Steve Martin) likes girl (Darryl Hannah), but the boy has a massive nose and fears the blonde bombshell won't give him a chance. So, he woos her with romantic poetry but asks his more handsome friend to take his place. She falls in love with the hunk's written words but not his actual "blah" personality. Can the boy really get the girl despite the deception? Yep! She can see past his ploy and his nose, and they live happily ever after! (Insert massive eye roll here!)

Splash—Speaking of the trend of casting the same actress, Darryl Hannah is back in this plot about a boy (Tom Hanks) who falls for a mermaid (Hannah). But when he meets her, she has legs, so he doesn't know the truth. She only turns into a mermaid when wet. It reminds me of *Gremlins* when all hell breaks loose when Gizmo is hit by water. Wait, where was I? Oh right, in the end, a boy can fall in love with a mermaid and live happily ever after!

Can't Buy Me Love—Again, I don't need to type anything about the plot 'cause it's the same as all of the others. Boy (Patrick Dempsey, a.k.a. *Grey's Anatomy's* McDreamy) is a loser who pays a popular cheerleader (Amanda Peterson) to be his girlfriend to up his cool factor. Naturally, she falls for him but really wants him to stay a dork 'cause opposites really do attract.

Overboard—I had to include this one as it has a special place in my heart and reminds me of someone dear to me. This one is a flip of the script. A wealthy woman (Goldie Hawn) comes into contact with a poor handyman (Kurt Russell), and they eventually live happily ever after! But she had to have amnesia (where she thought she was poor and already his wife) for her to actually give him a shot to begin with, otherwise she would have never looked his way.

I could easily include another dozen or so movies from the '80s with this same plot.

We get it. Opposites can totally attract and be together. Or is this just how it is in the movies?

I'm an '80's child, so I don't want to dissect this concept too much because I'm a hopeless romantic at heart. **But in reality, opposites CAN attract, but nine times out of ten, it ain't gonna work out, folks!**

In life, I've had many friendships where my hottie friend married the not-so-hot guy. He got insanely jealous because she was so pretty and attracted too much attention. His own insecurities took over, and well, cue the divorce.

Another friend married the guy who was poor, even though she came from money. Although a nice concept, they ultimately ended up divorced since that guy couldn't handle her wealth, and he couldn't fit into her life or societal demands.

And then I have friends who were dorky in high school but married the guys who were the "popular" jocks. The problems started when that awkward girl grew a rack and got gorgeous, but the "hot" dude just got fat and lazy! He made no effort, so cue the divorce.

And some are friends who were poor waitresses who married rich bachelors. They were usually cocky with inflated egos who abused their power. Insert the walking papers.

Don't get me wrong. It CAN work out. I'm just saying that after listing all these sappy '80's movies, we needed a dose of reality. Sometimes, it only works, until it doesn't!

Rescue your own damn self by attracting those with similar interests as you, from somewhat of the same social standing (or at least open-minded enough to evolve from it). Have realistic expectations as to how hard it is for those with tons of differences to actually make it work, and live sassily ever after!

If All Else Fails, There's a Show on Netflix to Distract You!

If life has taught me anything, it's that cable is something I can live without. Netflix is where it's at!

My name is Lori, and if you need advice on which series to watch on Netflix, I'm your go-to gal!

I may need an AA meeting to detox from the number of hours I've spent scrolling that app looking for the next binge-worthy, time-consuming mess of goodness.

The life lesson isn't that I can't get back all of that lost time, and I've been in some dark holes of "next episodes." It's this: **No matter how you are feeling in your life—good, bad, ugly, sad, happy, or mad—there is always a show on Netflix to distract you, entertain you, and make you go WTF!**

Let's prove a point on this one for those that aren't familiar with the whole craze of Netflix.

Scenario #1—You want to watch something totally different from what you're used to. How about wild animals and the wilder humans keeping them captive. Insert *Tiger King*. Suspected murder, criminal animal behavior, and years of questionable living arrangements (of both the tigers and their owners) make for some fucked-up viewing. My jaw dropped wide open at this unbelievable "reality" series! Picture mullets and missing teeth. Who knew people like Joe Exotic and Carole Baskin existed?!

Scenario #2—You want to play armchair detective by trying to crack a criminal's mind. Insert every single serial killer documentary or report on the murderer next door. Whodunits galore! Abducted in plain sight without a trace. What happened? Sit down in the safety of your home and watch the mysteries and trials of every infamous crime ever committed.

Scenario #3—You need to laugh? Well, look no further. From famous comics like Kevin Hart and Amy Schumer and Joe Rogan (my boyfriend!) to stand-ups you've never heard of but need to know (hello, my girl crush and dream best friend, Nikki Glaser), you'll be laughing your freakin' ass off for days (or weeks).

Scenario #4—Need a fix? From drug lords to the makers and the takers, there are documentaries, dramas, and even comedies about the dark world of narcotics on Netflix. Making pills, selling pills, taking pills, going to jail for it, then getting out and starting all over again! Lavish living and gritty survival are all intertwined in these addictive shows. I have watched so many of these, I think I'd be able to head up the drug cartel!

Scenario #5—"Celebs are my jam." Taylor Swift was one of my least favorite persons on the planet, until I watched a documentary on Netflix about her, and now I have mad respect, girl! Garth Brooks! Hillary freakin' Clinton! Lady Gaga! Michael Jordan! Tiger Woods! Get the "down and dirty" on all of your fav and not-so-favorite stars.

Scenario #6—"I need to release sexual frustration and be wowed with sensual, seductive, juicy, and provocative performances!" (Disclaimer: Ensure no children are awake or in sight while watching!) Seriously, who needs porn when you have Netflix?! And you can brag on social media you are watching all of it without the stigma attached to watching something X-rated. *Bridgerton* and its cast of smokin' hot actors was dubbed "mom porn" for a reason! Who knew an English period piece could be so racy? Have you tuned into the series *Sex/Life*? Holla! It made us allll want the 15 percent guy! (Or regret not picking him. #hadtowatchittogetit)

Scenario #7—If you need a distraction from everything and just want to watch shit that doesn't matter, there are plenty of choices. Like Gwyneth Paltrow's *The Goop Lab*. I wasted hours watching that series about nothing! And like the show about the founder of Bikram yoga and his disgusting ways. Netflix is a time-sucker for sure, draining the hours from your days and weeks, and sometimes, that's all you want (and need)!

Scenario #8—When you're snowed in or hiding under a blanket and don't want to leave your house, there are many series long enough to keep you company. My name is Lori, and I watched all of *Breaking Bad* on Netflix, all 61.3 hours, in less than two weeks! I'm not saying I'm proud of this, but I'm just saying it's possible. But the ultimate was when I decided to watch all of the seasons of *Grey's Anatomy*. I am for sure not proud of this one, but I am fully disclosing it here for the impact of what this chapter really is about. There really is something on Netflix to distract you from life's bullshit, always! At over 280 hours, it took me six weeks to get through. I promise, I was still a parent, walked the dogs, showered, and worked online for my clients, but it was not a pretty sight, and I for sure needed a meeting when that whole thing came to a close.

Yes, life is hard. Shit happens to us. Sometimes, we wanna scream and not go on. When you feel like that, grab the remote, scroll through Netflix, and find something to entertain and distract you.

Disclaimer: Do not confuse binge-watching with "Netflix and chill." If someone asks you to do this, there will be NO TV watching happening. #whoknew

Rescue your own damn self by becoming a Netflix addict like me, and live sassily ever after!

Failures, Grudges, Regrets...
Let That Shit Go!

....

Shit happens, babe, but you gotta move the frick on! Let that shit go! Legit, this was advice I once got from a very free-spirited yoga teacher: "Holding the weight of your past is too freakin' tiring and heavy!"

Once upon a time there was a girl named Lori. She lost hundreds of thousands of dollars on a fitness studio she opened and also lost her passion and ability to thrive. Lori lost weight, gained weight, tried fads, and crashed and burned. Lori was the queen of hating on someone and never letting them live down their mistakes. No forgiveness. No forgetting. One day, Lori chose to move ahead, to give up the madness of these fads, to forget the failure of the studio and loss of money and passion, and to allow people to get back into her good books. But did she really forgive and forget?

Ah, dwelling on the past. I swear if they gave awards for this, I would be on the top of that podium every single time. But after decades of holding that shit in me and letting it drag me down, I realized it was not only giving me wrinkles (and larger Botox bills!), it was just not serving me well in terms of my attitude. You see, we replay past mistakes over and over again in our heads, allowing feelings of shame and regret to shape our actions in the present. We continue to be frustrated about our past, while worrying about the future. We hold stress in our minds and bodies, which in turn can create serious health issues and so much tension. **We must stop allowing yesterday's stories to affect today's progress, because letting go of the past is necessary to truly flourish today.** Easier said than done!

We've all been hurt by others and by situations. It's part of life. And while the pain is often out of our control, I think it's helpful to remember that we CAN control how we respond to it and if we choose to let it go. Do we dwell on the past or do we learn what we can, then get back to the more important task of living life and moving forward? And how in the heck do we release, cut out, move on, and stop the madness of always thinking about the shitty things in our past? We usually bring it all along like heavy baggage.

Let's talk about grudges. A grudge is where you hold on to bitterness or resentment from past injury, pain, or trauma. Usually, it's something someone does or says, their words or actions, that we just can't shake or let go of. My good friend Mike once told me, "I used to brag and almost wore it as a badge of honor that I could hold a grudge better than anyone! Then I realized those grudges I was holding were all weight I was carrying. That in fact the other person had moved on, and I was the only one still harboring resentment, thinking about that situation, stressing about it! I was waiting for an apology or for them to ask me to release it or forgive them, when I was actually the only person holding on to it. THEY had moved on! I thought there was unfinished business by holding the grudge, but the other person had closed that business down for bankruptcy long ago!"

Letting go completely often means forgiving the person in your own mind. You don't even need to bother texting or calling them 'cause they've likely forgotten about it long ago. Forgive them, release the negativity or feelings around it, then move the heck on!

Regrets are like assholes—everybody has one! They're because of missed opportunities and being disappointed that something didn't result in a different endgame! We all make mistakes! *What the heck was I thinking?!* is something I used to ask myself over and over again. I was the regret queen! Now, every time I'm about to board the "regret" train, I stop and question what the scenario taught me. What did I learn because of that regret? I remind myself that I'm wasting my time dwelling on it and tell myself, "Hey, girl, that sucked, but it's okay."

Life has crappy moments, and eventually they're gonna teach me something!

"I'm such a failure!"

I loathe this word. I used to walk around thinking the opposite of success was failure. Umm, that's not true at all! I used to try to hide my failures or missteps. Push 'em deep down and hope no one noticed I wasn't "perfect!" I started to look around and hear others promoting their failed attempts. They were wearing that failure badge with pride by accepting that shit happens and that sometimes, it doesn't end in that success. **It's okay to fuck up and have it not work out!**

I met a woman who had been married three times, owned multiple empires that crumbled, and went from riches to rags. Olivia was such a talented and positive woman. I couldn't comprehend how happy she always was. I mean married and divorced three times! Failures! Four massive corporations that flourished, then she lost everything to bankruptcy, and now she works for her family business. She had a massive house in downtown Vancouver worth millions, then moved to a little one-bedroom condo in a shady part of town. When my studio failed, I kept that nightmare with me as "failure" baggage for years until Olivia helped me change.

"Lori, those marriages were all amazing at the time. Full of life and love. They weren't failures. They taught me what I want and what I don't want. Those businesses that I grew to massive numbers gave me the strength and smarts I still carry with me today. I loved my times running them. When they didn't keep rising, it was time for my next chapter. Having a lot of money taught me how to make that money again, if I want it. Every step and moment in my life brought me to today. If I think of them as bad or failures, then I won't ever try or jump again. It would be very sad if I stood still with fear by thinking of the past and holding onto it!"

Rescue your own damn self by letting go of the grudges, regrets, failures, or missteps, and live sassily ever after!

Ditch the Debbie Downers!

My girl Britney Spears wrote all about the toxic shit we have to endure. #freebritney

Toxic people suck! They drain the energy from us.

Negative Nancy.

Troubled Tammy.

The "sky is always falling" type people.

Like the poisonous apple Snow White bit!

Like the venomous juices a wicked snake bites into ya with!

Destructive.

Harmful!

Dangerous! Just plain unsafe to be around!

Life's too short to always be thinking the worst of everything. Life passes by quickly, more so when we don't make the most of every single experience. I don't know about you, but when we get out of the pity party and navigate our way out of the swamp that is negativity, life is just so much more sassy and magical!

Maybe you're a Debbie Downer or maybe you're surrounded by too many friends or family members who are pessimists who suck out all your positive energy and weigh you down with worry. Either way, that shit isn't helping you rise. Nor does it make you feel sexy or badass. So, it's time to let that go! Like really, LET IT GO!

I had a friend, who, no matter what positive thing you said to her, would respond with a negative retort. "Hey, Shelley, you look like you lost weight, good job!"

"Well, I'm still ugly!"

Legit. *That* would be how she took the compliment.

"Wow, the sun is shining so bright. It looks like the best day out there today!"

"Well, I heard rain is coming tomorrow for a month."

Like tell me you're not drained by simply reading that. Do you have any people in your life like this? Imagine hearing that every single day at your workplace or at home. Perhaps it's you, your partner, coworker, family member, or friend who always behaves in this manner. Energy—positive or negative—is contagious. Misery loves company, but that company doesn't need to be you!

Cut ties and get rid of this badass energy before you are sucked dry. Because before you know it, your mind will start to think the same way. Jim Rohn once said that we're all the sum of the five people we spend the most time with. Whether these are people in real life or people on your social media feeds, if they bleed you dry every damn time, they've got to go! Cut that cord and keep your energy, your vibes, and your whole life clean and impactful!

Your time is precious, and life is too short to always be trying to pick everyone up around you. Choose wisely who gets your time.

"My attitude is the size of my ass! You've been warned." I have this printed on a sweatshirt. Love it! My attitude is a positive one, and I found the saying so funny. You see, I always try to spin it and turn a negative into a positive. I try my hardest to see the rainbow after the storm. I try my best to laugh when times get tough.

I know we all have tough times that are absolute shit, but in the end, surround yourself with a Positive Patti. (Sidenote: Patti Lewis is my bestie, so I had to drop her name AGAIN 'cause she's one of the biggest rays of positivity I know! Love you, Patti!) Now, I'm not one for toxic positivity. You cannot just affirm or use crystals and bath bombs to get out of some incredibly fucked-up situations. Nor can you make it through by numbing your emotions. I mean, you might make it through for a short time, but eventually, it will catch up with you. And you'll be forced to deal with it. So, you might as well surround yourself with people who've fully got your back, who love you, who are positive, hopeful, and who know that every step always feels that much better when you have someone cheering you on, especially on days when you don't see or feel it yourself. These people are your rays of sunshine. If you don't have a "hype squad," get yourself one ASAP! I'm fuckin' serious! It's life changing!

I have a client, Shannon, who is full of sunshine. She's super positive. I was complaining to her one day about this stretch of a terrible flu I had. It was like ten days of throwing up, aches, and pain. I felt like complete shit and sent her a complaining text: "I am so sick of this flu. I feel like ass. Life sucks . . ." The text went on and on.

Her only response was this: "Well, at least you still have nice lashes!"

Unfortunately, she had an allergy to the glue and hers had just been taken off . . . and she looked like an alien (been there, it ain't pretty!). We still laugh our asses off to this day about it, because in that moment of feeling like complete garbage and thinking my world could be ending, all I needed was that funny, uplifting, positive person to turn my frown upside down. It made a world of difference.

I mentioned my best friend, Patti, who I lovingly call Positive Patti because she is always lifting me up and making me smile. I remember complaining to her about the heartache I was experiencing at the time. And her response to me: "Well, you're hot AF, so fuck the world!"

Another time her response was: "You are a queen, and no one deserves you!"

My friend Christina (didn't change her name 'cause she loves owning this one) uses a tough-love approach. Most of her positive texts are more like: "Babe, you are smarter than this. You need me to come over there and bitch-slap you?" See, positivity comes in many forms!

The messages my friends send me are always those that lift me up and never push me down. Get yourself a girl gang who reminds you of your power. Who sees you for who you are. Who will fight for you like hell. Who will lift you up when you feel down. Who will embrace your crazy with you. And who will bitch-slap you with positivity when you need it!

Be that person who reaches down to your friends in their sadness and lifts them up. And make sure you always have these types in your corner. There is no time in life for the downers and the energy suckers.

Rescue your own damn self by breaking free from the negativity of others and adding more positivity to your own actions and outlook, and live sassily ever after!

Pretty Woman

A modern-day Cinderella story, where a streetwalking, broke prostitute (Julia Roberts is back again in another unrealistic, hopeful romantic comedy) meets a high-powered, rich stud (Richard Gere). These two fall for one another, and against the odds of thinking these two worlds could ever collide, it works out, and they live happily ever after! Nope, not buying it! Although after I first saw this, I did think, "Wow, everyone can meet their prince, and he won't care if you're a sex worker because none of that matters in love." Yeah, right!

Listen, I actually don't want to rip this one apart too much. I want to believe they can and will end up together in the end. But I also want to believe in more than just him rescuing her. At the end she says she rescues him too! I do believe in life, with our partner, it's all about give and take. Giving and receiving. Mutual respect, trust, honesty, communication, love, and kindness. Mutual back-scratching, my friend!

In this life lesson, let's rewrite *Pretty Woman*.

Pretty Couple

Vivian (Roberts) is rescued from a life on the streets and selling her body for money by Edward (Gere), but she saves him from a loveless life that was all about money and work. So, they both kinda rescued each other from a life of being abused by money and power.

Way too deep, Lori! Stay with me on this one, though. I like to believe we all have talents and abilities, but sometimes money, or the lack thereof, holds us back from pursuing some pretty badass things. So, in this revamp of their story, Vivian is smart, funny, witty, and talented. She goes on to do amazing things, beyond just happy times with Edward. Maybe it works out for them, maybe it doesn't. But I changed the narrative to make it all about her being able to do some great things even though her life hit some tough times before. We've all been at that broken and helpless stage, and by we, I mean me! Sure, I haven't had to sell my body for money on the streets, although that "onlyfans" page has sounded tempting or necessary at times! We've all spiraled down and have needed that wicked opportunity to jump back up to the top.

For most of us, this upswing doesn't involve a rich guy finding us on the streets of Hollywood in super uncomfortable black thigh-high boots! Usually, we have to find ways to turn it all around on our own. We have to rescue ourselves from the streets of despair and the bad wigs and tight barely there clothing! #whenyaknowyaknow

In the end, this movie still gives me hope that **anything is**

possible. Hello, you've already been sold on the "hooker plus rich guy equals fairy tale ending." If we bought this concept, we could buy anything! Don't underestimate yourself and just how badass you are. Don't doubt your gifts or the power you have when you truly get your mind behind something. You can make anything you want happen!

Sidenote: Best word ever used in this movie: "Cinder-fuck-in'-rella!" I use it weekly!

When the going gets tough, believe in your own talents, use your own resources, and don't settle or give up when the cards are stacked against you. No matter what your situation, lace up those hooker boots, rescue your own damn self, and live sassily ever after!

Remembering Is the Best Medicine!

....

Just because they aren't next to us, doesn't mean they aren't WITH us!

Losing someone to death is so difficult. Losing someone is hard. Loss is loss. Grief is grief. There is no minimizing it. We've all experienced loss to some degree in our lives. Maybe it was the loss of an older relative when you were younger. My grandfather passed away when I was in my late teens, and that was the first time I truly experienced what death and loss was. I had gone with my parents to funerals years prior, but my emotions couldn't process what was really happening. I remember seeing people crying, telling stories of remembrance, and my empathetic self would be sobbing, too, but I didn't really understand why.

Little did I know that the first time of feeling loss would not be the last. Life is about losses: tragic ones that we can't explain, ones that come out of nowhere and kick us square in the gut, and ones that continue to make us tear up just thinking about them.

But in my life, I can say this sure as day, **remembering heals us during times of loss**.

The people I would see at funerals when I was a kid, who were telling old stories about their friends or family members who had passed, were using memories to mourn, to grieve, and then to start their healing.

Now, any time I see someone smoking I think about helping my grandfather roll cigarettes that he would chain-smoke in the corner. When a Johnny Cash song comes on the radio, I think of my grandpa and how he would tell me stories of Johnny like they were old war buddies.

I've had friends pass away in tragic accidents, then I would get together with my closest circle for an almost party-like atmosphere of remembering them. We would tell stories about our lost friend, crying but also healing through laughter and reminiscing about the great times we had.

My great friend Sandy, who has suffered too much loss in her lifetime, was remembering her son Daniel (remember the rock bottom with no bottom?!) who died so young. She once said to me, "I believe that rainbows are people shining down on us. I believe somewhere they are all watching out for us."

She told me this because when she was sitting in sadness in her kitchen one day remembering how much she missed her son, crying, a small rainbow peaked through the window and onto the chair beside her.

"Rainbows are now how I feel I'm with my Daniel again, like he's here beside me."

Now, every single time I see a rainbow, I make sure to

remember someone I've lost to death and say a little hello to them and their colorful hugs and kisses!

The loss of a pet is another heartbreaking experience. One of my dearest friends Kevin lost his precious dog (I can't watch *Marley & Me* to this day again because I sobbed so hard). I have two dogs now, and it angers me because I know one day I'm going to have to experience that loss. When that happens, I'm sure I won't be able to speak for weeks. Trust me on that! When Kevin had to say goodbye to his Boxer, Stella, it was tragic. For years, just saying her name brought out the waterworks. On the second anniversary of her passing, I sent him a blanket with a pic of her on it, and a photo album with a collage of her photos. More waterworks. As I apologized over and over again for causing this extreme pain and upset, he said to me, "No, Lori, this isn't pain and sadness, this is remembering. I had so many good times with her. Seeing these pictures brings tears for sure because I miss her, but I am thankful I had her, and the memories are all of happier times."

In trauma, I take comfort in the belief that those we have lost are somehow here with us. Some might believe in Heaven; others believe in reincarnation. Some think there are souls in the air all around us, looking out for us. Others believe those souls are inside us. Like when a person does leave this earth, maybe we get to keep a little part of them in our hearts. When we have no strength to get through something difficult, that little part of them is cheerleading for us, bringing out the sword to nudge us to keep fighting our dragons. Hang on to those parts that make you feel warm, like they're still here with you.

Rescue your own damn self by never forgetting those you have lost; keep faith they are still with you somehow. Honor them, talk about them, take little signs that remind you of them, and don't let go of their love. For then, we are never really slaying the dragons on our own, as we have our own little warrior gang inside us and around us helping us to live sassily ever after!

Pets Are Life!

....

My name is Lori, and I am obsessed with dogs!

My teens make fun of me and are so embarrassed by my ability to make out with any dog I see in public. #noregrets #yolo If I see you with your new puppy outside a store, I won't leave your side until I've gotten about sixty-five billion puppy kisses, found out your dog's name, weight, breed, age, and how well they are coping! My daughter always says, "Mom, legit, you asked them if the puppy is sleeping through the night. STOP! You are so embarrassing!" #truestory

Dogs are life to me!

Now, for some people, this might not come in the form of a dog; maybe you're a cat person (you are not on MY team, but hey, you're still on a team!). I have friends who are parrot people and friends who are snake people. Whatever floats your boat. Any animal will do and make sense with this storyline.

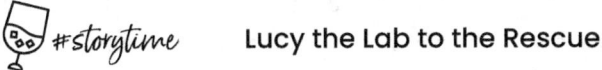 **#storytime**   **Lucy the Lab to the Rescue**

Character outline: Lucy, a female Labrador Retriever, and Sasha, a forty-plus female human.

Now, this pretty lady was not just any average lab. She had a white face with bright eyes that said, "I am so freakin' cute!" The way she walked and carried herself was so unique. She was clearly the best dog on the planet! Truly! I'm not biased!

Sasha adopted this princess at nine months old from the breeder, and so began their beautiful lifelong friendship. Soon after Lucy came into her life, Sasha suffered a stroke (at a very young age), which required a long recovery and time away from work. Lucy was by her side the whole time.

Lucy was also there when Sasha's eleven-year marriage crumbled, and you better believe she made damn sure she got the dog in the divorce. Take everything else, take the shirt off my back, take the sports car, but "I GET THE DOG!" She needed to start all over in love, but she had her amazing Lucy on her team!

Sasha is a super neurotic gal who loves routine, just like Lucy. They made the perfect team. Morning walks, dinner at 5 p.m. sharp, and evening ball throws in the backyard. Lucy even helped her to deal with a long-distance romance for almost a decade. With her soul mate and love across an ocean, she had Lucy's daily comfort and companionship to help fill a void. Heck, some would say Lucy was her bestie and her life partner! She would look at any guest who entered Sasha's apartment, like "When ya gonna leave me and my bestie alone, strange person?" Or "Hey, you're sitting in MY spot on the couch." Legit, she was the queen of that house, for sure, and rightfully so!

The physical benefits of having a pet are great because rain or shine, these fur babies demand daily walks, which means you also get your daily exercise in. And the emotional connection we feel with animals is even more powerful. They give us comfort, trust, and respect. Sasha had Lucy to snuggle with during those quiet nights, and she provided mental stability too. Life is freakin' hard, and as energetic and crazy as dogs are, Lucy brought this sense of calm, allowing my friend's very busy brain to just shut off and be. I don't think I've ever seen a picture of Sasha without Lucy in it. When Sasha was exhausted after a long day of work, she'd lie in bed and decompress by petting Lucy for ages before they both fell asleep.

Lucy also taught Sasha about loss. In March 2019, our dear Lucy left us all for doggie heaven unexpectedly (RIP, sweet girl. I know she's up there searching for her stuffed squeaky toys, chasing balls, or snoring in her sleep).

For any of us who have lost our best friend, it's a long journey of grieving and dealing with the trauma surrounding their loss. It's difficult being alone again and learning to live with the fond memories of someone you've lost (yes, I consider dogs to be people, sorry, don't fight me on this). Losing a pet does prepare us for handling the loss of actual real humans. For anyone who has kids, you will understand this. Once a child has lost a pet, it's not as foreign or as "out there" when they lose their grandparents, since "Grandma is now in Heaven walking Lucy." Losing a pet can remind us how to hold on to memories. Being able to talk about them after they are gone and remember the good times they provided, helps.

The love of an animal knows no boundaries. Animals don't ask for much. Feed me, walk me, love me—that's it! In life, everyone else takes so much from us. Humans have hidden agendas and self-absorption that pets just don't.

Pets also give us comfort. When I was injured and had foot surgery, my goldendoodle, Sadie, didn't leave my side. She knew I was hurt and laid next to me for six weeks while I recovered. When I was dealing with insane bouts of anxiety, it was my labradoodle, Sam, who became my "anxiety dog." Sitting next to me, with his head on my lap, he helped to calm me more than any medication could have! (Disclaimer: I don't think pets should replace meds. Trust your doctor on this one.)

Rescue your own damn self with the assistance of a pet's love (dog, cat, horse, elephant, goat, whatever!), and live sassily ever after!

"Marvel" at Your Own Superpowers!

Get it? Marvel? Anyone?

Wouldn't it be nice for me to write a chapter where we are all allowed to use superpowers to rescue our own damn selves? Where we become superhuman superheroes who can save ourselves from the madness and depths of despair?

If only it were that easy.

But wait, maybe we are all born with gifts of superpowers.

What if we are all our own sassy superheroes? I did make a pretty sexy Catwoman for Halloween 2001!

Stick with me here. I know, yawn, Batman bores me, especially when it's Ben Affleck playing the character; give me Christian Bale any day! Mmm, dark caves and tight rubber . . . Wait, what was I saying?

A superhero is someone who does thoughtful, impactful deeds and has the ability to help others with talents or "powers" that not everyone else has.

Show of hands if you have a preteen boy who still spends endless moments trying to explain that Batman isn't a Marvel superhero, he's a DC Comics character, and without catching his breath, proceeds to list every hero in each of them for the next four hours! #idontcare

I want you to think about your superpowers. What are you exceptionally great at? What is something that you can do so well, you could do it with your eyes closed? Is there something that you are frequently asked about—advice, guidance, help? Dig deep and discover your superpower. It's your magic. I believe us mere mortals all have 'em!

Maybe we don't even realize we have them! Maybe we are Clark Kent just working away at the local newspaper, and it takes some kid falling into Niagara Falls before we realize we can fly to save him! Just sayin'!

Maybe it's not that you can fly or see through metal or telepathically transport yourself to the beaches of Greece to see your bestie! I've thought this one through a lot, clearly.

I've wanted to have invisibility as a power many times when my kids were driving me batshit crazy! Oh, to just disappear!

Telekinesis is about moving objects with your mind. I sometimes sit and think, *Garbage, take yourself out!* and I turn around and it's gone! (Perhaps it's a superpower and not my fifteen-year-old doing it to earn his weekly snacks! Or maybe it's a mixture of both. You attract the vibes you put out there. You know, the whole "law of attraction" thing!)

Telepathy is communicating with someone with your mind. This is something I KNOW I have. I can just give my kids a look, and they know they better get their laundry off the floor and clean their rooms. It's a gift I have! People can look at me, and with my mind, not my resting bitch face, they just know it's not a good time to talk to me!

Anyone who has gone through vaginal childbirth gets to say they have superhuman strength as their power! I had an eleven-pound baby with NO DRUGS! Just try and argue THAT wasn't something that required hero status!

Every day, we put on makeup and shapeshift ourselves into looking like someone else. If ya have seen me without makeup, Botox, and my lashes, you know the transformation I'm talking about!

I am a professional multitasker who can get shit done in record time—perhaps speed is my superpower! Although not actual running, bleh, I am not even a speed walker on that front.

My friend Sandy and I swear we are psychic, not to be confused with psycho, which some would also say describes me! I know you are pregnant before you do. I can feel goosebumps and this weird feeling when something bad is gonna happen. I am not gonna go out there and say I can predict natural disasters or claim that I see dead people, ew, no. I am not Whoopi Goldberg's character in *Ghost* talking to the dead Patrick Swayze character. I just feel stuff. A sense. A sick sense (not sixth, it's sick. I also have a really dirty mind!).

I can cross the line as well in saying my superpower is

clairvoyance also known as ESP (extrasensory perception). Those who think I had to Google this must not have a preteen boy. Trust me, many dinner conversations revolved around him educating me on this shit! #truth Seeing the future. I can see when someone is a jerk or is gonna be a jerk, yep, called it, he is a jerk!

Some people's sense of smell is so strong, they can taste what they smell. Ew, that wouldn't always be good. It's called "clairgustance," and it's a thing!

There are so many other potential superpowers that this topic could be its own book that no one would read except my fifteen-year-old son!

I'm saying we all have our own versions of human superpowers. Whether we choose to use them for good or evil is our own choice. If I could see through stuff y'all better believe you would find me outside Mark Wahlberg's house checking out what's under his Calvins! Don't knock it, you know you would be there too!

Rescue your own damn self and own the things about yourself that are your talents, abilities, and superpowers, using them for good and not evil, and live sassily ever after!

The Wizard of Oz

This doesn't look like Kansas anymore!

Girl and her dog take on the land of Oz! Sign me up for any adventure that includes my dogs by my side!

My name is Lori, and I have watched this movie sixty-five billion times! I know every line, every song, every moment! I've had nightmares of flying monkeys picking me up and kidnapping me for decades now!

Lori's *Fast and Furious* Fairy Tale Breakdown:

* **Dorothy** is on a farm in Kansas, with her trusty dog, **Toto**, of course! Every good story has a girl and a dog!
* A tornado comes and takes her house away and it lands in the magical Oz! But her house crushes and kills the Wicked Witch of the East (not to be confused with the Wicked Witch of the West, a.k.a. ME when I let myself get too hungry or overtired!).
* Dorothy meets the one good witch, who sends her to see the **Wizard** (hence the title, *The Wizard of Oz*!), so he can help her get back to her family and farm!

* On her adventure down the yellow brick road, she meets three strange men: the **Scarecrow** (who doesn't have a brain), the **Tin Man** (who doesn't have a heart), and the **Cowardly Lion** (who doesn't have courage). So they join her to go ask the Wizard for these things too!

* On their travels to see the Wizard, the real Wicked Witch of the West (not me) is trying to sabotage them 'cause she's ticked off that Dorothy killed her sister with a flying house!

* They meet the amazing Wizard who (spoiler alert) has no powers at all and is a fake and phony (like most people on social media these days!). But he gives the Scarecrow a brain (really just new sticks and needles for stuffing); he gives the Tin Man a silk heart stuffed with sawdust; and the Lion gets a special potion of "courage." Really, it's him tricking them into believing for themselves. They had the things they needed within themselves all along!

* He tries to take Dorothy home to the farm in his giant air balloon, but it breaks. American Airlines wasn't flying to Kansas that day!

* Eventually, the good witch tells Dorothy that she has the power within her to get herself home. She just has to click her heels together three times and

say, "There's no place like home, there's no place like home, there's no place like home!" The lesson being, your mind is powerful. Your thoughts are powerful. The intention and emotion behind them are powerful. So step up that self-talk, sister!

✳ It was all a dream! Dorothy wakes up in her bed with her family around her and Toto by her side. She was home all along.

The Facade or Complete Insanity in a Nutshell:

✳ Okay, so this whole movie is indeed a facade: flying houses, munchkins, witches, and a talking tin can. It was clearly meant to be a dream, so I can't rip apart any of it! It just works! And it's so fun to believe! It's completely insane 'cause it's supposed to be wild crazy talk!

Lori's Revamp of this Madness—*The Wizard of Oz*. Nope, I can't do it!

I can't dissect this movie! Unlike all of the other fairy tales where I had witty ways to make it more realistic or believable or legit, I want to keep this one in *Oz* land! I like living in the belief there is a yellow brick road! And I want those sparkly red shoes, damn it!

What I can do is take my own little life lessons from this movie:

* Courage—Just like the Cowardly Lion, we all have courage. Life scares us, shit goes down. We need to face it and realize when the little mice try to scare us, we are freakin' brave lions! Know that inside, we've had the courage in us all along!

* Smarts—Just like the Scarecrow, we all have brains, wisdom, and knowledge. Some of us might have a little more stuffing up there blocking it than others! Life is about taking the things we are good at and using our "tools." Life is about Googling the shit we don't have any knowledge about or "phoning a friend" to help tutor us! Or hiring some help! Being smart isn't just your IQ, it's about taking your wit and your brain and knowing you are one Miss Smarty Pants!

* Love—Just like the Tin Man, we all have a heart and are capable of love and deep emotion. Life clouds this with darkness and hate sometimes, and we become cold like tin. But if we can oil that sucker up, we can remember to lead with our hearts!

* There is no place like home—sure, we can enjoy packing the bags and heading for the hills on lavish vacations. But home is our familiar location, loving

environment, and safe space. It doesn't have to be a house with four walls. Home can be a person who makes us feel safe, secure, and loved. It could be a feeling of comfort within ourselves. It's fun to want to escape. Heck, life makes us want to run away at times, but home is the best place to be.

Dream the dream of colorful rainbows, shoes that sparkle, flying houses, witches and wizards, the excitement of yellow brick roads, and dancing little people. But in all of the magic, at the end of the day, rescue your own damn self in knowing there's no place like the comfort of your own home, your own peeps, your own self, and live sassily ever after!

Let's Get this Show on the Road: I've Got a Date with Matt Damon!

....

I know I've got to write a conclusion, an ending to this book, *but I don't wanna!*

I hate the word "conclusion" because it literally means THE ENDING.

And, babe, ***this* is just the beginning of your epic adventure.** Of your twisted and tantalizing "fable" of life!

Forget ending this! We are just getting fuckin' started!

Before I get kicked off the stage at a bad comedy club, I just have to thank you for reading this book. Thank you for choosing to reclaim your story and regain control of your own narrative in your own fairy tale called "life." Thank you for taking the time to look for other ways to navigate this crazy world and for letting go of the need to always feel like you are barely keeping up with the Kardashians!

Thank you for knowing it was time for a change, time for a movement in which we, as women, can come together and finally give up this charade of trying to fit into a mold we were never meant to fit into or by believing the chronicles telling us we're supposed to be rescued by someone else!

Thanks for knowing we need to live every day like it could be our last! Embrace the good, the bad, the ugly, and everything in between! All of it! Why live if we aren't truly living?!

If you could take just one thing away from this book, I would love for it to be this:

You deserve to FREAKIN' RESCUE YOUR OWN DAMN SELF! Drop the mic!

You deserve to unlock the handcuffs we have all been in for so long, this prison that says we are waiting for someone to set us free!

You deserve to make mistakes and not beat yourself up for them.

You need to dust yourself off like Cinderella when she lost that damn slipper and keep running—in comfy sneakers 'cause who is running in high heels anyway? (Besides Carrie Bradshaw in *Sex and the City*!)

I get it; life is freakin' hard! But what if we found ways to make it a little *less* hard? What if we found ways to soften the blow of this craziness by not believing the bullshit we're sold?!

What if our storyline could be one of a beautiful baby growing into a strong little girl, a kick-ass teen, then an adult woman who takes all that is thrown at her, makes it her bitch, and has the most badass life ever!

We aren't promised sunshine, roses, and rainbows every day! But taking it one step at a time, day by day, and trying to make the smaller moments count, wouldn't life just feel better?

I used to try to fix the crowns of the babes in my squad around me, my clients, my friends, my Starbucks baristas! I used to think that by drawing my sword, I could fight the dragons for them!

But the answer is allowing each and every queen to own the crooked crown she sports and slay her own dragons! **We all have the power within to be the master in our own kingdoms!**

This is your time to start a new chapter in your own heroic tale of life!

Take your body, every inch of it, and create what you want to create. Be who you want to be. Rock the moments. Sink into your struggles and make your story one of the legends. Be the queen in the tower, who not only saves herself, but saves her prince and the whole damn kingdom!

It's okay to be the princess sobbing in the corner for a day or a week when life gets too hard. It's actually normal to not have it all figured out and have times we lose shoes and just say fuck it, "I'm going to bed to sleep this one off!"

It's okay to NOT search for some outside person to fix us, save us, rescue us, and to create some happily ever after for ourselves! Lessons, fairy tales, and romantic comedies can actually send us a message if we truly read between the lines!

We might meet our Jerry Maguire, and we might just "complete" him, but we might feel incomplete and keep searching for our own "Sexiest Man Alive!"

Our faraway tower might just be a detox from the world we needed, resetting our mentalities until we are ready to join the human race again!

Just like Dorothy and Toto, we are making our way home, to ourselves, and finding out we have always had the courage, smarts, and heart all along to get this shit done ourselves!

Once upon a time there was a badass babe who didn't take shit from anyone!

Who said it like it was.
Who didn't care what others thought.
Who kicked ass in this thing called life (Dearly beloved . . . Prince, anyone?).
Who loved being naked.
Who had an unlimited number of orgasms.
Who was happy and kick-ass in her being.
Who made light whenever she could.
Who slayed the haters (a.k.a. dragons).
Who knew not to drink the poison (a.k.a. social media and society bullshit).

This goddess came, she saw, she conquered, and she grabbed the hands of all the other babes in the

kingdom too. They all learned to speak their truth, always!

In the end, she RESCUED HER OWN DAMN SELF and LIVED SAS-SILY EVER AFTER!

Like a Bad Oscars Speech, These Are My Thank-Yous, and I'm Bound to Forget the Most Important Peeps!

I have so many people to thank on this journey to release the book. And like that moment when I am standing in front of the world trying to remember those who helped me on this quest, I will draw a blank and miss thanking someone special to me (you always forget the most important ones!), so I am just gonna say sorry if I missed ya right now!

Thank you to all of those I have crossed paths with throughout my years. Men. Women. Those who loved me, those who challenged me, those who hated me and helped me grow. I fuckin' LOVE YOU ALL!

To my clients, and anyone from my past who has shared their stories with me (whether you know it or not, don't worry, I changed your names!). By being so open and raw with me, I was able to bring this book to light. Thanks for being in this fairy tale adventure with me!

Thank you to the amazing babes in my life who know who they are. My besties, friends, posse, girl gang, and hotness community! I am surrounded by the most amazing peeps. You have genuinely made me a better person—and possibly an alcoholic—and I love ya! You are all top-notch and my queens! Thank you to Asha for being another set of eyes on the final polishing of this book!

Thanks to my kids for blocking me on social media years ago, so they wouldn't have to see the madness of their mama's posts. Or me in lingerie photoshoots or worse, buck naked! Thanks for accepting that your mom is a little "out there" and in the public eye, probably saying the lamest things. But you still love me! Brooklyn and Beckham, you are both amazing souls, who teach ME the lessons of life! In my fairy tale, YOU are both my happily ever after!

To my amazing publisher, Sabrina, words can't express how you waved your magic wand and made this book happen. Wait, maybe you are my Fairy Godmother after all! You made ME rescue myself!

Tania, my editor. You are the sidekick friend in all the comedies, in all the messiness with the lead actress, making sure she shines bright!

Kelly, my other editor, who scared me with 1812 old-school fairy tale fables, but reminded me of the good witch who helped Dorothy get home (and who knows how to research all things romantic comedy and fairy tale!).

Doris, I think you are like Tinker Bell in *Peter Pan*, who was watching over the interior design of this book—and just making it burst with magical pixie dust!

Christine, you were more of the "tough-love" editor fairy, the magical knight who rides up on the white horse near the end to save the day!

To P, the problem with you is . . . actually, I don't have time to list all the problems, it's "ten minutes till Wapner!"; "I'd rather be nowhere with you, than somewhere without you!"

Last, but not least, thank you to ME! Yep, I'm thanking myself. Heck, I rescued myself from that sobbing mental mess I was, and I was able to rise to be the queen who could save herself! It's been a very tough life so far, and it won't get any easier! I could have stopped and said "fuck it" many times. I could have curled into a ball and assumed the cards were stacked against me. I did this often, but I always got back up! The tears I shed just made me stronger. So, thank you to myself for GETTING THROUGH STORMS and RESCUING MY OWN DAMN SELF! I am owning my fairy tale, writing my customized romantic comedy (I would like Ricky Gervais to play my love interest and Pink to play me!), my own dreams are being surpassed, and I am a fierce golden knight slaying any dragons in my way!

xoxo
Lori

Required Viewing

Fairy Tales

Aladdin (Ron Clements, director, 1992, Walt Disney Pictures)

Cinderella (Clyde Geronimi, director, 1950, Walt Disney Pictures)

Snow White and the Seven Dwarfs (David Hand, director, 1937, Walt Disney Productions)

Tangled (Nathan Greno, director, 2010, Walt Disney Pictures)

The Little Mermaid (Ron Clements, director, 1989, Walt Disney Pictures)

The Princess and the Frog (Ron Clements, director, 2009, Walt Disney Pictures)

The Wizard of Oz (Victor Fleming, director, 1939, Metro-Goldwyn-Mayer)

Rom-Coms

27 Dresses (Anne Fletcher, director, 2008, Fox 2000 Pictures)

50 First Dates (Peter Segal, director, 2004, Columbia Pictures)

Can't Buy Me Love (Steve Rash, director, 1987, Buena Vista Pictures Distribution, Inc.)

Dirty Dancing (Emile Ardolino director, 1987, Vestron Pictures)

Eat Pray Love (Ryan Murphy, director, 2010, Sony Pictures Entertainment)

Four Weddings and a Funeral (Mike Newell, director, 1994, Rank Film)

Jerry Maguire (Cameron Crowe, director, 1996, Sony Pictures Entertainment)

Maid in Manhattan (Wayne Wang, director, 2002, Sony Pictures Entertainment)

Notting Hill (Roger Michell, director, 1999, Universal Pictures)

Overboard (Garry Marshall, director, 1987, Metro-Goldwyn-Mayer)

Pretty Woman (Garry Marshall, director, 1990, Buena Vista Pictures Distribution, Inc.)

Pretty in Pink (Howard Deutch, director, 1986, Paramount Pictures)

Roxanne (Fred Schepisi, director, 1987, Columbia Pictures)

Runaway Bride (Garry Marshall, director, 1999, Paramount Pictures)

Say Anything (Cameron Crowe, director, 1989, 20th Century Fox)

Sixteen Candles (John Hughes, director, 1984, Universal Pictures)

Sleepless in Seattle (Nora Ephron, director, 1993, TriStar Pictures)

Splash (Ron Howard, director, 1984, Buena Vista Pictures Distribution, Inc.)

The Breakfast Club (John Hughes, director, 1985, Universal Pictures)

The Wedding Singer (Frank Coraci, director, 1998, New Line Cinema)

Wedding Crashers (David Dobkin, director, 2005, New Line Cinema)

When Harry Met Sally (Rob Reiner, director, 1989, Columbia Pictures)

Movies

Annie (John Huston, director, 1982, Columbia Pictures)

Batman Begins (Christopher Nolan, director, 2005, Warner Bros. Pictures)

Forrest Gump (Robert Zemeckis, director, 1994, Paramount Pictures)

Ghost (Jerry Zucker, director, 1990, Paramount Pictures)

Kindergarten Cop (Ivan Reitman, director, 1990, Universal Pictures)

Marley & Me (David Frankel, director, 2008, 20th Century Fox)

Mean Girls (Mark Waters, director, 2004, Paramount Pictures)

The Green Mile (Frank Darabont, director, 1999, Warner Bros. Pictures)

Thelma and Louise (Ridley Scott, director, 1991, Metro-Goldwyn-Mayer)

The Sixth Sense (M. Night Shyamalan, director, 1999, Buena Vista Pictures Distribution, Inc.)

Crime Shows

America's Most Wanted (1988–present, 20th Century Fox)

Criminal Minds (2005–2020, Disney Media)

Dateline (1992–present, NBCUniversal Television)

Law & Order (1990–2010, NBCUniversal Television)

Netflix

Breaking Bad (2008–2016, AMC)*

Bridgerton (2020, Netflix)

Gray's Anatomy (2005–present, Disney ABC Television)**

Sex/Life (2020, Netflix)

The Goop Lab (2020, Netflix)

Tiger King (2020, Netflix)

*available on Netflix

**up to season 17 available on Netflix

Classic TV

Beverly Hills, 90210 (1990–2000, CBS Television)

Charlie's Angels (1976–1981, Spelling-Goldberg Productions)

Dallas (1978–1991, Warner Bros. Television)

Dancing with the Stars (2005–present, BBC Studios)

Dawson's Creek (1998–2003, Sony Pictures Television)

Dynasty (1981–1989, CBS Television)

Friends (1994–2004, Warner Bros. Television)

Gray's Anatomy (2005–present, Disney ABC Television)

Happy Days (1974–1984, CBS Television)

Melrose Place (1992–1999, Worldvision Enterprises)

Saved by the Bell (1989–1993, Rysher Entertainment)

The Bachelor (2002–present, ABC Television)

The Brady Bunch (1969–1974, CBS Television)

The Dukes of Hazzard (1979–1985, Warner Bros. Television)

Three's Company (1977–1984, Fremantle)

Lori Mork is more than just a sassy best-selling author.

She's got BABE communities spanning the globe.

To get in touch with Lori for empowerment and life coaching,

check out her website: https://www.lorimork.com/

For some witty, comical, and just plain raw (and real) content,

follow her on social media: 📷 @lori.Mork;

ⓕ lorimorkcoach

To book Lori for appearances or speaking opportunities, fill

out the contact form on her website or message her directly

at lori@lorimork.com

Rescue Your Own Damn Self

EMPOWERMENT & LIFE COACHING

https://www.lorimork.com/

📷 @lori.Mork

ⓕ lorimorkcoach

Lori Mork is a fierce and dynamic best-selling author, kick-ass motivational speaker, and empowerment and life coach who has helped thousands of women worldwide reclaim their lives, own their truth, and step into their power by sharing her own authentic story unapologetically. She helps you bring your sexy back—deep within your mind and body and in relationships with others. A lover of unlimited Pinot Grigio (with ice), Lori is your "good times" gal, your older sister preaching all things advice, and your mama bear who always has your back all rolled into one feisty and fiercely loyal friend who is not afraid to lay it on the line: "Life's too short to feel like shit! Why stay trapped like some helpless damsel in distress when we already possess all the tools to escape and create our own sassy fairy tale!"

YGTMedia Co. is a blended boutique publishing house for mission-driven humans. We help seasoned and emerging authors "birth their brain babies" through a supportive and collaborative approach. Specializing in narrative nonfiction and adult and children's empowerment books, we believe that words can change the world, and we intend to do so one book at a time.

🌐 ygtmedia.co/publishing

📷 @ygtmedia.co

𝐟 @ygtmedia.co

www.ingramcontent.com/pod-product-compliance
Lightning Source LLC
Chambersburg PA
CBHW061135120626
46546CB00005B/1787